"This is a record of how 'church' h
isn't looking – how people are gath
by the sheer force of the Spirit's lead
us in mission – not least in commu
about, or even don't much want to ____
inspiring testimony to God's creative liberty at work in our times."
Dr. Rowan Williams, Archbishop of Canterbury

"Martin tells a very moving story of discovering where God is at work in mission and following where he leads. It is significant that the resulting fresh expression of church among the Romany community in Kent stretched him to new understandings of mission and the church and to rediscover practices for identifying and developing indigenous leadership. We believe these lessons are transferable to many other mission contexts in our plural culture today".
Bob & Mary Hopkins – National Fresh Expressions Team

"It is such a moving story on a number of different levels. Firstly, it opened my eyes about the Romanies themselves. Secondly, it is the story of a ministry which is constantly awakening to new depths of revelation of God's love. Thirdly it is an epiphany of the length and breadth of God's grace and his work amidst all the vanities of the human condition. Praise God!" Bishop Michael Turnball

"As the Romanies began to share their stories, many of us found ourselves in tears as we realized our own poverty. They were such a blessing to us in bringing us back to hear from God. For 'God chose the foolish things of the world to shame the wise; God chose the weak things of the world to shame the strong.' We heard the challenge to lay down our cleverness and pride and come in simplicity, as these wonderful people had. On Sunday we truly saw the power of God at work and seeing that has challenged us to come back to simple faith in Jesus."
Revd Shiela Porter, St George's – Deal.

"A charming and moving story of what happens when a vicar welcomes a group of travellers who believe in the miraculous into an ancient village church where the parishioners believe in the pews."
Jonathan Gledhill, Bishop of Lichfield.

THE PURE IN HEART

AN EPISTLE FROM THE ROMANIES

MARTIN BURRELL

authorHOUSE®

AuthorHouse™ UK Ltd.
500 Avebury Boulevard
Central Milton Keynes, MK9 2BE
www.authorhouse.co.uk
Phone: 08001974150

First published by AuthorHouse 6/9/2009

ISBN: 978-1-4389-8821-4 (sc)

ISBN: 978-1-4389-8821-4 (sc)

This book is printed on acid-free paper.

"I consider all that I have written to be mere straw
compared to what has now been revealed to me."[1]
Thomas Aquinas

ALL PROFITS TO THE ROMANIES

---

[1] Towards the end of his life, on 6th December 1273, after celebrating Mass on the Feast of Nicholas, Aquinas gave up his writing saying these words. He died a few months later.

Contents

Chapter One

The Light from the Tower

Cranbrook, Kent, England

Christmas 1998

"The people walking in darkness have seen a great light;
on those living in the land of deep darkness
a light has dawned."[2]

Rachel and Moses

Shortly after I began work as vicar of Cranbrook in 1999, Derek, an enthusiastic member of the local free-church, urged me to visit one of the local Romany families to hear their story. I didn't really know what a "Romany" was back then and was curious to find out. I rang the doorbell and Moses and Rachel welcomed me into their home. The fact that I was the local vicar seemed important to them and Moses immediately began telling me of his experience of Christmas Eve, 1998. Late in the evening he had been sitting in the sitting room when

---

[2]   Isaiah 9:2

1

he suddenly became aware that the whole room was full of dazzling bright light, with a particular focus of the light on the couch on which he was sitting. The light appeared to be coming from outside their home. Moses approached the window and stood for a time simply marvelling at the brightness of the light streaming into his home. After a time, he went outside into the dark cold of the night to investigate. There was no obvious source of the light, like a lamppost that might have suddenly turned on. As he looked beyond their neighbourhood towards St Dunstan's, he became aware of a powerful beam of light that was shining straight down from the tower of the church and into their home. After a while he went back into the sitting room. The light filled the room for about half an hour and then disappeared.

Moses repeated the story several times to me with Rachel from time to time encouraging him to keep going. I think they were aware that I was struggling to understand their strong Romany accents. When I then echoed back to them Moses' experience, they seemed delighted that I had understood and that I was taking them seriously. I sensed that they were hoping that I might be able to offer some kind of illumination of the experience. After all, I was the vicar.

I had, at that time, a sense of awe. We were about to cross the threshold not just into a new century, but into a new millennium. I felt nervous and anxious to be cutting my teeth as a vicar at such an historic moment. I took Moses' experience away with me and asked God to reveal to me its meaning. In my sermon at midnight mass that Christmas I explored with the congregation whether this was a sign from God. Was he on the move in the same way that he had been when the angels appeared to the shepherds on the hillside, announcing the birth in Bethlehem of the Saviour? Not one person spoke to me after the service about this and so I took Moses' story and treasured it privately in my heart.

Today, some nine and a half years later, I have come to know Moses and his family well and he has given me a fuller account of what had been happening in his life back then. For a whole ten years, right up to his Christmas Eve experience, Moses had been unable to sleep at night for any more than two hours. He had been prescribed pills but to little avail. Finally he gave up the pills and continued every night to simply cry out to Jesus to deliver him from his insomnia. From the night of the shining light from the tower until this day, Moses tells me he has slept every night like a baby.

I am now certain that the experience of that night was a prophetic sign pointing beyond itself to an outpouring of God's love on the Romany people of Cranbrook. At the first Christmas, God had singled out the shepherds as the ones who would be first to hear the Good News of the newborn King. At Christmas 1998, God had singled out the Romanies to be the first to learn of an awakening of faith that would come to our town. When Mary had accepted that she had been singled out to be the mother of Jesus, she understood that God was ushering in a radically new order. She sang…

"He has performed mighty deeds with his arm;
he has scattered those who are proud in their inmost thoughts.
He has brought down rulers from their thrones
But has lifted up the humble." [3]

---

[3]   Luke 1:51-52 *from the Magnificat, the Song of Mary.*

Chapter Two

Vicarage Holly

Christmas 1999

As we were settling into life in the vicarage that same winter of 1999, the doorbell rang one afternoon and my two teenage daughters, Rebecca and Naomi, answered the door. They came back into the house to let me know that a young girl was there, asking for "olly". After a bit we worked out that she wanted some holly from the vicarage garden to make wreaths with. Her confidence endeared her to us and she explained that in the car down the drive, was her partner, Roy and their first baby, a boy. Once dad had collected some holly, they told us that they had been "converted, but not baptised". By now they had worked out that they had called at a vicarage and that I might be disposed to performing the ceremony of baptism. Our daughters were struck that the young woman was only a little older than they, and yet she was already a mother.

Christmas 2000

Exactly a year later the same young woman rang the bell and asked for some holly for the Christmas wreaths. We remembered her from the previous year and were pleased to oblige. As we got chatting we explained that since her last visit I had become ill and had just had an operation for bowel cancer. Her news was that in the car down the drive were now two sons being looked after by dad. The demand for family baptism was growing and so I promised that, once I was back at work, we would press on and organize the ceremony. At that point I had no idea that it would take three operations and six months of chemo to rid me of the cancer and that I would not be back to work for a year and half.

Christmas 2001

When the young family called in the run up to the following Christmas I was in convalescence and feeling extremely fragile, only too aware of my own mortality. By now we knew the young Romany woman as Pashey, her partner as Roy, and her sons as Roy and Jasper with an Aaron on the way. The need for a family baptism was growing by the year and the family was aware that, if I were going to be there for them, God would have to step in. Pashey told us how she had been praying for my healing all along and that she had been given a picture of me being held in the wings of an angel as I was going through my ordeal. This touched me profoundly, for I had preached on Psalm 91 a few days before my first operation:

> "Surely he will save you from the fowler's snare
> and from the deadly pestilence.
> He will cover you with his feathers,
> And under his wings you will find refuge...
>
> ...For he will command his angels concerning you
> to guard you in all your ways;
> they will lift you up in their hands,
> so that you will not strike your foot against a stone."

Holly was duly collected on that visit and Christmas was at celebrated at St Dunstan's in my absence. Then, in January 2002, I returned to work, grateful for every day God might grant me to live and determined to do everything I could to advance his Kingdom in Cranbrook.

2002

By now Pashey, Roy and their rapidly growing nest of sons had been moved from a gypsy caravan site in Ashford to settled accommodation in Hawkhurst, a few miles from Cranbrook. Plans began to take shape for a family baptism and in 2003 Roy, Pashey, Roy, Jasper and Aaron were all baptised at the new 11.15 Sunday service. There was great joy that their deepest desire had been fulfilled.

Roy & Pashey and their five sons - 2008

Chapter three

"Lustig ist das Zigeuner Leben

faria, faria ho!"

As a child growing up in Harlow, Essex, I knew very little about gypsies. They had set themselves up in caravans not far from where we lived and tethered their ponies along the side of the roads near us. The general view was that these were a strange people who were to be feared and who had no right to be living in our neighbourhood. Every now and then someone would blame the disappearance of something on the gypsies. I was careful never to cycle down the lane where they camped and fearful that, if I did, I would be attacked by violent men and dogs. I never actually met or even saw a gypsy. An irrational prejudice and fear had been successfully instilled in me.

However, when on family holidays in Switzerland, we would sing together a song about them as we drove along in the car.

"Lustig ist das Zigeunerleben, faria, faria ho!"

I had just enough German to know that we were singing something about the joyful life of the gypsies. But I struggled to equate this with the image I had been given of them back home as a dark, mysterious and dangerous people. My real acquaintance with Romany-gypsies only began here in Cranbrook all these years later.

Once Roy and Pashey Smith and their boys began coming regularly to our new 11.15 Sunday service I realized, that there was really only one way of getting in touch with them midweek, and that was face to face. If there was a change to the time of service - which happened quite regularly - I would be able to let the regular congregation know about this quickly through a group email message, the magazine or, as a last resort, by a text or telephone call. However, the only way to let the Smiths know about anything at all, was to pay a visit. For several years this meant a fifteen-minute car journey to Hawkhurst. Later, when the Smiths were re-housed in Cranbrook, it meant cycling up the hill to their home.

In the early days I used to be quite irritated at this inconvenience but, gradually, I began to notice a curious thing happening. I would arrive at their door flustered, weighed down with too many ministerial tasks to accomplish, and keen to get back to more important matters as quickly as possible. But something was beginning to change within me. Whether or not it suited me, forty-five minutes in the Smith home required me to enter a world radically different from my own. In their home there were no clocks or watches, no papers, pens, diaries, computers, emails, mobiles or phones. There was, in fact, no information available other than what was spoken and no agenda whatever other than the agenda of the moment. Sitting and simply being with them forced me to confront my own drivenness and tension. My life had become a life of projects, deadlines, agendas, meetings, minutes, rotas, occasional offices and diary events. Theirs was a life of freedom and simplicity. I remembered the song of my childhood *"Lustig ist das Zigeuner Leben!"* *"Joyful is the Gypsy life!"*

One experience in particular stands out clearly in my memory. I had asked Roy to drive me over to my parents' home in Harlow to pick up a couple of beds and bring them back to Cranbrook. Over the course of the two hour journey I began to notice that my cares were very slowly beginning to slip away and that I was actually rather enjoying the whole outing. It occurred to me that whilst, for me, the agenda was successful transport of furniture, for Roy there was no agenda other than the chance to spend time with me. I felt honoured, loved for who I was rather than for any way I might be useful. I noticed that, while I was continually glancing at my watch, anxious to achieve as much in the day as possible, for Roy there was simply no concept of the passage of time. *Chronos* time, time that can be measured by hours and minutes, did not exist for him. There was only the present and the ever-real possibility of something unexpected and remarkable happening within that present. Out of the blue experiences - *kairos* moments - such as Moses had had that Christmas eve, were part of the everyday fabric of life for Roy and his people, something normal and to be expected. My life, meanwhile, had become so busy and so ordered that little room was left for such luxuries. However passionately I might preach on Sundays about God intervening supernaturally in our lives, the truth was that these Romanies knew far more about this than I. With some horror, I realized that I had been hard-wired into modernity. My trip with Roy was the day on which I began to seriously wonder whether my own culture had led me up a blind alley.

> "Surely everyone goes around like a mere phantom;
> in vain they rush about, heaping up wealth
> without knowing whose it will finally be."[4]

All kinds of bells began to ring for me. Around that time I had began to explore resonances between post-modern theological insights and the writings of pre-modern writers. Medieval texts like *"The Cloud of Unknowing"*, the writings of people like Julian of Norwich, Meister Eckhart and Thomas a Kempis, were beginning to touch my soul. At theological college they had not been regarded as serious theology and were relegated for use on quiet days when our heads were granted permission to have a few hours rest. Now, whilst fully engaged with the day-to-day reality of parochial ministry, I had begun a serious search to re-locate my heart. Reading Melvyn Matthew's book *"Both Alike to Thee"*[5] had set me off on the right track. It began to feel exciting to be alive at a time when the four hundred year legacy of rationalism, of which I was a product, was beginning to collapse. I realized that I was caught up in a widespread search in the Western world for a recovery of all that has been lost from our culture over the centuries.

As Roy and I drove on our way I found myself thanking God for bringing this man into my life. I began to wonder whether his illiteracy and lack of education was, in fact, a mercy. Roy was simple but very deep. I had become complex yet very shallow.

---

[4] Psalm 39:6
[5] Published 2000

Chapter 4

"Martin's become all emotionable"

July 2006

The Smiths settled into life at St Dunstan's and, after a few years and the birth of a few more boys, Pashey and Roy began to think about getting married in church. They explained to me how, within Romany culture, a man and a woman who had privately pledged themselves to one another, were regarded as married; to violate the pledge would have serious repercussions within their community. At St Dunstan's we already thought of Roy and Pashey as Mr. and Mrs. Smith but, nonetheless, they felt that, if they were to become more fully integrated within our culture, this would be an important step for them to take. After all, strictly speaking it was unnecessary for Jesus to submit to baptism at the hands of John the Baptist, as he was already without sin, but he had chosen this path in order "to fulfil all righteousness". Morally speaking, Roy and Pashey had already tied the knot, but to set the right pattern for others, and to be the full shilling within the eyes of state and church, they asked me to marry them.

The ceremony was planned, guests were invited but, a few days before, we had to cancel as the boys went down with chicken pox. A new date was agreed and a whole host of Romanies from across Kent swept into our church carrying masses of lovely food for the reception in church. Since they didn't have two ha'penies to rub together, they had decided to do the whole thing themselves. The church was filled with an amazing sense of fun and freedom. Formality seemed an entirely alien concept to these people: they only did spontaneity. Once everybody had rolled up, we got the ceremony on the road.

I had conducted eighty or so weddings by this time and felt I could do them in my sleep. However, something happened during the liturgy that day which had never happened to me before. We had come to the exchanging of rings. The Church of England tradition is well known: the priest reads the words line-by-line, prompting first the man and then the woman to repeat the same words. In our literate culture this always feels a little unnecessary, but Roy needed me to say the words for him and I was reminded of earlier generations when many in the community would not have been able to read.

"Pashey, I give you this ring as a sign of my love."
"Pashey, I give you this ring as a sign of my love."

Having completed this opening sentence and heard Roy say the words after me, I found myself unable to go on. I simply starred at the next line I was to supposed to read:

"All that I am I give to you, and all that I have I share with you".

I looked up at Roy. Here was a man wanting to give the whole world to his partner. All that he had, he was determined to share with her. But he had nothing to share. He had no wealth, no education, no degrees, no possessions, no status. The only thing he had to give, was himself. Roy's gift of Roy to his beloved was worth little in the eyes of our culture but, in the eyes of his God, it was worth the whole world. His gift to her was unconditional.

It was for me as though the whole meaning of love was distilled down into that moment. Many a couple had stood before me over the years, each conscious of their individual contribution to the marriage and what might be in it for them. But here was a man, who had not even had the chance to forfeit his soul in order to gain the whole world. He stood before his Pashey empty-handed.

Something was stirring in my heart, but in a place deeper than I knew existed. An incredible joy was rising up within me, partly because I knew it didn't matter a hoot if I cracked up altogether. I think the man in the parable who stumbles across hidden treasure whilst digging in a field must have felt something like this. Surprised by joy. Aware that what he had discovered was worth giving the whole world for.[6]

Tears were dropping down onto my liturgy as I stood, speechless, before the couple. I looked up at Pashey. I think maybe she sensed what was going on for me. Time stood still. The congregation waited. God didn't seem in a hurry.

---

[6] Matthew 13:44

After a time I found myself able to continue. But it wasn't as though I had pulled myself together. Rather it was as though I had gently let go of one world and was about to take my first step into a new world.

"All that I am I give to you, and all that I have I share with you".
"All that I am I give to you, and all that I have I share with you".

Together we began to roll again. Rings were given and received. In my homily I lined all the Smith boys up next to me and shared the story of the vicarage Holly with everyone. We had a lovely lunch together and I went around chatting with the guests unaware at the time, that within a few years, I would come to know them all well.

In theological college the kind of experience I had that day is called a "critical incident". One is encouraged to be a "reflective practitioner" and to take time out to process what has happened. At one level, this was God breaking into my liturgical auto-pilot and shocking me out of what Max Weber has called "routinized charismata". Every vicar who gets into a rut, and finds himself just going through the motions, needs a good shock like this from time to time. But now, as I look back over this experience in the light of all that subsequently happened, I understand this *kairos* moment at Roy and Pashey's wedding as a moment of conversion. At theological college in Bristol the pastoral theology tutor, Sue Rose, had told us, quite robustly, that there were two kinds of conversion. The first conversion was to Christ. The second was to the poor.

Chapter five

The Burning Bush

Charlotte

After some time, it dawned on me one day that Roy and Pashey were related to the other Romany family I knew in Cranbrook. Moses, who – right back in 1999 – had told me of his experience of the light from the church tower, was Roy's brother and he and his wife, Rachel and their family were now living over the road from Roy, Pashey and their boys. After a little encouragement from Pashey, her sister in law, Rachel, had started to come to church from time to time. Her children - Charlotte, Annie, Mary and little Moses - would also come along occasionally. Big Moses was pretty resolute that he had no need to go to church since God was already in his heart. I didn't push the matter. But he seemed, at the time, to be a man looking for a purpose in life.

One Sunday in the early summer of 2008 during our 11.15 service, I noticed that Rachel was quite animated, beckoning me over to where she was sitting in the pews. Somehow, it seemed more important to go and find out what this was about than to stand up front singing. Something significant had clearly happened at Rachel's home and she was eager to tell me, in the hope that I could offer some explanation. Later that afternoon I popped up the road to hear from Charlotte and her mother, Rachel, what had happened. This is what they shared…

A few days earlier Charlotte had come back home to Goddard's close with her Aunty Lottie. It was 11pm and so quite dark and quiet. Charlotte noticed, on getting out of the car, that a bush in front of the house was on fire. Approaching the burning bush she became aware that it was not being consumed by the fire. After a few moments, a pillar of golden light arose from within the bush, rising to a height of six feet. Charlotte stood and watched this extraordinary sight for a few minutes until the pillar of light moved off into the sky and disappeared and everything returned to normal. Lottie had not been conscious of any of this, as though the sight was not meant for her.

Meanwhile, that same night, unbeknown to Charlotte, her mother, Rachel, had an extraordinary experience too. She had been lying awake in bed when she became aware of the sound music. She described it to me as "religion music". Wondering if anyone had left any CDs playing, she went downstairs to check. Everything was off. The music continued to play and Rachel realised that this must be music from heaven, the sound of angels singing.

The next morning, mother and daughter shared their experiences of the previous night and were in awe. As they told me their story, I realized that Charlotte had never heard the Bible story of Moses standing before a burning bush that was not being consumed by the flames[7]. She had heard nothing of the Lord's call on Moses' life to deliver his people from slavery in Egypt and bring them into the Promised Land. We all marvelled at this, not least since her dad's name is, of course, Moses!

This was the kind of thing I had read about in many a Christian biography and I had always wondered if I would ever be caught up in revelations like this. The fact that Charlotte and Rachel are two very down-to-earth and well-balanced women caused me to take their experiences seriously. I shared what they had told me with others in

[7] Exodus 3

church, but I was greeted with the same silent response that I had faced when I shared Moses' story of the light from the tower shining into his home.

Some months later, I asked the Romanies what they thought the meaning of the burning bush and the religion music was. It was little Roy Smith, aged 10, who raised a hand and said: "God has drawn near to us."

Chapter six

Naturally Supernatural

Increasingly, I had the sense that God was up to something significant in our little community of Cranbrook. Burning bushes and heavenly choirs were the kind of thing that happens in the Bible and that one reads about in Christian books. But now it seemed to be happening both under my nose and within my own heart. God was indeed drawing near. It was as though his hand were reaching down and very gently touching us.

I was deeply struck by the way the Romanies were dealing with these phenomena. I was tempted - like any success-hungry vicar - to jump into the nearest pulpit or up onto the nearest rooftop to capitalize on the story as quickly as possible. I yielded quickly to this temptation and now regret not allowing God to be God and take care of his own publicity. Meanwhile, I noticed that within the Romany families there was a complete absence of hype. To them, the burning bush and the "religion music" were quite normal things to be happening. They felt no need to get hysterical, no need to look in the mirror to see if they had a more sanctified look, no need to report to the Bishop. I was also struck by the complete absence of scepticism. Charlotte and Rachel had been keen to check out, carefully, whether what had happened that night could be explained in some natural way or, alternatively, whether they were losing their minds. It was important for them to establish that these phenomena were of supernatural origin and not figments of the imagination. Rachel, for example, had made a point of checking carefully that no sound equipment had been left on in the house. And I noticed something further. There was, for them, not a whiff of "this kind of thing doesn't happen". I began to wonder whether "this kind of thing" doesn't happen to most of us because our world-view is closed to the supernatural. These Romanies were the most naturally supernatural people I had ever met. For them there was no line in the sand dividing the natural and the supernatural. God was for them all in all, constantly revealing himself in all manner of ways.

There was something else that I began to treasure very deeply. There was in my new friends a total absence of cynicism. Not once did anyone in these large, extended families feel the need to mock or to explain away what was happening. Within my culture we use humour to make everything safe and predictable. Our collective body language betrays a need to keep everything well under control, especially God. Our need to keep a tight rein on when, how and where events take place, has the effect of marginalizing the One who comes and goes, not according to our agendas, but like the wind. We may preach and teach about the sovereignty of the Holy Spirit, but our culture keeps her conveniently caged. I began to wonder whether God had been able to step into the lives of these Romany families, simply because the doors of their homes and the windows of their souls were wide open to him. But was there, perhaps, a far more important explanation?

Meister Eckhart said that when God comes across a heart that is truly humble, truly empty, then He has no other choice but to fill that heart to overflowing. When a people has been marginalized for six hundred years, vilified and made the scapegoat for the ills of a society, as the Romanies have been, then they are left very humble and lowly of heart. God is unable to fill a mouth that is already full or speak into a heart that is already satisfied. But these people were hungry for God and for purpose and meaning in life. So he appointed a beam to shine from the church tower into one of the most humble homes in Cranbrook in 1998. And ten years later in 2008, he appointed a bush to burn outside their home and angels to sing within it.

Chapter seven

The Kindling of Vision

By early 2008, I had started to pop in to spent time with my Romany friends on a weekly basis. By now, I was no longer motivated to visit in order to impart information about a parochial event. I wanted to be with them because it had become one of the very few places in Cranbrook where I could chill out and be myself. Walking up the road meant walking past the newsagent's where, quite commonly, a billboard would be announcing the latest twist in the row going on in our church over the pews. The word "vicar" was usually there in large letters and, over the period of a few years, I had become the focus of some media attention. The church and the town were divided over this matter and it had all become very unpleasant. By virtue of their culture, the Romanies were able to carry on their lives almost completely oblivious to town politics. There were, therefore, two narratives unfolding for me at one and the same time: the Romany narrative and the Ecclesiastical narrative. At the surface level, these two narratives were quite independent of each other. At a deeper level, I was carrying the joys and the agonies of each in my heart every moment of every day.

"Praise be to the Lord,
for he showed me the wonders of his love
when I was in a city under siege." [8]

One day, I was in Roy and Pashey's home, when Roy began to tell me that he had plans to build a big shed in his garden for the Romanies to meet in, a shed equipped with a wood-fired stove to keep us all warm and to cook on. Though glad to have the comfort of a house, those of Roy's generation who had known the nomadic life found it difficult to be stuck in one place and indoors. The shed might restore something of the old life that they had forfeited and, above all, it would be a common meeting place. Roy is not a man to exaggerate or to have unrealistic ideas, so when he told me that large numbers of Romanies

---

[8] Psalm 31:21

would be coming to worship God together in the future, I felt I should take what he was saying seriously. He explained that his family was linked into a whole network of relations right across the South East and that they were really like one large extended family. I remembered his wedding guests and recognized that the potential was certainly there.

The vision for a garden shed fellowship, however, was not to be. A year earlier in 2007 Roy and Pashey had hosted a gathering after an 11.15 Sunday service and the garden was full of a whole host of people from St Dunstan's. It was a truly blessed occasion when all the normal cultural and ethnic barriers were down and we transcended ourselves, dancing and singing together and enjoying Roy's outstanding wood-fired barbecue. This had been for me a window into how I have always imagined heaven to be. Away from the holy ground of the church building, all things become possible. There were no pews to prevent our dance and no eggshells on the ground to tread on. Nonetheless, all things may be possible in the back garden of Romany family, but not all things are permissible.

Serious complaints were made to the local housing authorities and Roy and Pashey were told that, if anything like that ever happened again, they would be moved on from their home and not given new accommodation. The final nail in the coffin for the idea of garden-shed fellowship came when they were told that planning permission to construct anything in the garden would be not be granted. I shall never forget Roy's sense of powerlessness and hurt.

At that time I became aware, that one of the deepest longings of the Romanies was to be able to meet together regularly and without threat. Whilst the rest of the community was free to enjoy all manner of gatherings in each other's homes across the Weald, the Romanies were issued with warnings when too many people came to visit them. Moses' family was even accused by the authorities of living at another Romany home in town other than their actual address. Not a shred of evidence was offered in support of this.

Until now, the Romanies had kept this darker dimension of their existence from me. But, now, I was beginning to understand that racism has followed them to every country in which they have tried to settle. Was there, I began to ask myself, more to the burning bush than I had realized? This was a people in need of liberation from captivity. Yes, God had drawn near to them. But what were his plans for them?

I suggested to Roy and Pashey that, if there was no mileage in the garden shed, then we could meet at Church House, right next to the church. We agreed to explore this idea further with Moses and Rachel. At that time, I had been learning a lot about cluster-sized groups as a means of growing the church from the grass roots up. And so the idea of an homogenous Romany cluster was born in my heart. I determined to find a way of providing a place where they could gather together to worship in their way, and at a time that suited them.

Chapter Eight

Pastor Lywood

Goudhurst 1960-1995

As we began to dream dreams and see visions, my new Romany friends started to tell me about a man who had played a key role in their past and who they continued to revere. This was Pastor John Charles Lywood. His story is quite remarkable. Out of the top drawer and educated at Eton, he had served as a bombardier in World War II completing 49 operations and receiving the DFC. Amazed to be still alive, he became an extremely successful businessman and made his fortune. However, one day whilst driving across Kent on business, he saw the sky open before him and Jesus appear. Jesus said to him "blessed are the pure in heart".

Lywood stopped at the next telephone box, told his secretary that he had finished work for the day, and drove to a Christian bookshop to purchase the best Bible money could buy. He went home and searched in his new Bible for the words Jesus had spoken to him. Before long, this conversion experience had led him to spend time with the down-and-outs under Charing Cross bridge in London. By the late 1950s, he had set himself up as a free church pastor, gathering together the locals in Goudhurst.[9] He felt God begin to call him out of his comfort zone and into the local fields where the Romany gypsies had settled. He found himself praying for a Romany man whose wife had just left him and their children. On returning the next day, Lywood discovered that the wife had returned from London and all was well again.

The Romanies took Lywood to their heart and began attending his church, which met in Goudhurst village hall by the pond. His ministry to them was powerful and prophetic. Conversion was taken very seriously and former practices had to be renounced before baptism would be granted in a tiny little room at the back of the stage where Lywood had introduced a bath. Candidates would go through one door into the back room and, following full immersion baptism, would re-enter the hall through another door that gave onto the stage.

Moses in the room where Pastor Lywood used to baptise.

---

9   Goudhurst is 15 minutes drive west of Cranbrook.

Over a period of 25 years, Lywood baptised hundreds of Romanies, some of who travelled to his church from across Kent. At his retirement in 1995 the village hall fellowship became unsustainable, in spite of the fact that Lywood had made efforts to train up Romany leaders to succeed him.[10] However, the fellowship Lywood had begun and that had borne such fruit in his day, became a memory that Romanies treasured in their hearts and often spoke of.

As I got to know the Romanies better, I became aware that they had learned much of their spiritual language from Pastor Lywood. I remembered how Pashey had told me, when she first called at the vicarage for holly, that she had "been converted but not baptised". Others used similar phrases and there was a lovely commonality to their spirituality. Those old enough often told me about Lywood and his willingness to go the extra mile for his people. It became clear to me that, whatever God might be beginning in Cranbrook, we were only building on what this man had done a few decades earlier. God had intervened in his life and opened his eyes to see Jesus; and this had lead to him to encounter Jesus in the most needy and marginalized people of the community. His ministry to the local residents did not bear the fruit he had hoped for and he felt called to turn his attention to the poor. Were these Romanies the "pure in heart"? Were these the ones whom Jesus had spoken of on that day when he had appeared to Lywood in the sky? How did this verse go on? "Blessed are the pure in heart *for they shall see God."*

As I got to know these extraordinary people, I felt a new kind of love welling up within me, a love of a kind that I had never experienced before. From time to time, over the years, I had seen this kind of love in a few people and felt very humbled and inadequate. I had seen it in the eyes of a monk I had met one day as a theology student in Bristol. He was spending most of his time with the drug addicts and alcoholics in town[11] and I had not forgotten the extraordinary effect meeting him

---

[10]   Roy and Moses' bother, Aaron, is active in ministry in East Sussex.
[11]   He was one of the "Little Brothers of Nazareth" who work near Bristol bus station. They spend five hours a day contemplating Christ before they begin their work!

had had on me. If I had kicked him hard in the shins, I felt quite certain that he would still have gone on loving me and accepting me without condition. However, sixteen years after meeting him, I had finally come to the conclusion that I would not be granted this kind of compassion for others and would have to remain a mediocre minister.

At first I was quite shocked to discover such feelings of compassion arising within me. Although not trained in anatomy, I think I might be able to pinpoint the actual locus in the body. Was this the "bowels of Christ"?[12] The underlying Greek for "compassion" in the New Testament is "splaxna" which means "bowels". A third of mine had been surgically removed in 2001; now, in 2008, it felt as though they were being spiritually re-instated! My healing from cancer had been pure gift and I experienced every day of life as such. Now, I was discovering compassion in my heart as a gift of pure, unmerited and unearned grace. There was more treasure buried in the ground than I had bargained for and, once again, I felt like selling everything I had, in order to buy the field in which this treasure was hidden. I wondered whether it was a similar experience that had led John Lywood to give up all his wealth and status to be with the Romanies.

Whilst writing this account, I read the autobiography of Bruce Olson in which he tells the story of his call to leave a potentially glittering career in academia to bring the Gospel to the Motilone Indians of Columbia.

> "Why should I have to work with naked, starving people?" God
> never told me why. But He did change my heart. Gradually my
> pleasant dream of becoming a linguistic professor vanished into this
> ridiculous idea of going to other countries to talk to savages about
> God. I knew it wouldn't make sense to my parents; it didn't even
> make sense to me. But over the months, as I walked to school,
> as I sat and daydreamed in class, as I read the Bible, he gave me
> something I'd never bargained for: *compassion*." [13]

---

[12] Philippians 1:8 μαρτυς γαρ μου εστιν ο θεος ως επιποθω παντας υμας εν σπλαγχνοις ιησου χριστου "The bowels of Christ" KJB
[13] Bruchko - Bruce Olson 1973 page 27 (my italics)

As I witnessed the gradual rekindling of faith in Jesus amongst the Romanies, I continued to marvel at the sheer simplicity of their encounter with God. Their culture enabled them to be "pure in heart" in a way that seemed closed off to my own people. Their purity of heart made it possible for them to "see God" in a way that seemed to elude my people. My new Romany friends, from the babies to the oldest, constantly communicated to me how much they appreciated what I was doing with them. I knew well what familial love was from my own lovely family. But the love and acceptance I received from them would at times overwhelm me. "Martin's getting all emotionable" eighteen-year old Charlotte would say when I became tearful. These Romany homes were becoming places of light and solace. Anyone stepping across the threshold could be themselves, free from any causes to win, free from any issues to sort, free from the need to prove anything to anyone. I knew that, the moment I stepped back into my role as vicar, I would be reduced to an ecclesiastical construct and would cease to be Martin. As one Gypsy prayer from Albania puts it, "a land without Gypsies is a land without freedom."

Chapter Nine

A Romany Cluster

Spring 2008

Once it became clear that Roy's garden shed was not to be, I suggested to Roy and Pashey that we meet in Church House once a week. I explained that whilst the Sunday 11.15 service was where we did church together with others from my culture, it would be important for the Romanies to gather together where they could do things their way.

Right back in the 1980s when still working as a musician in Glasgow, I had relished reading Vincent Donovan's "Christianity Rediscovered. *An Epistle from the Masai*". By now this had become a seminal work in missiology and I was fully aware of the imperative of allowing the Gospel to find expression in ways that were relevant to each culture on earth. Donovan took the Gospel to the Tanzanian Masai tribesmen, learning their language and allowing them to discover ways of expressing the Gospel from within their own culture. Once he had done this he moved on, giving them the freedom to ordain their own leaders and live out the Gospel in their own way. Roland Allen had commended this approach as early as 1912, calling the church to have a fresh look at the way St Paul had carried out his missions.[14] But few got it. Here at St Dunstan's we had got it, and had come to recognize that birds of a feather do indeed flock happily together. Accordingly, we had created three distinct Sunday morning tracks of worship and linked these to several homogenous cell groups. We had found that it simply does not work for one group to impose their style and agenda on another from a different cultural background. And, all along, I was continuing to discover, at a much deeper level, just how radically different Romany culture is from my own. Their need to meet as a discrete group became ever more urgent.

We agreed that our Romany cluster would meet weekly on a Friday evening at 6pm. We got the word around and all was made ready for our first meeting. By around 6.40pm the first began to arrive. I made

---

[14] *"Missionary Methods. St Paul's or ours?"*- Roland Allen, 1912

a pact with the Lord. I would not allow anything to upset me or deter me from pressing on with the vision. When the dears arrived it was hugs all round. Then we got going with the programme for the first session. I had had some success using the *Journeys* DVDs from New Zealand with a variety of different groups in church. This course is entirely testimony-based with a strong emphasis on the supernatural. The four or so Romanies who came along to those first sessions loved to hear stories of God's intervention in everyday lives and they shared their own, often remarkable, testimonies quite naturally. The absence of embarrassment and scepticism came as a wonderful counterpoint to the extreme difficulties people from my own culture experience in finding a place for the supernatural within their worldview.

Not that we were without our own problems. Romany families arrive within their own *kairos* understanding of time. When I ask them if they are planning to come along to an event they always respond "Yes, Martin, God willing!" When I reply "I think He is willing," they don't get my kind of humour. Why should they? After all, they don't do cynicism. The wonder of their approach is that, when they do roll up, it's not because the clock has told them to, or through any sense of guilt or duty; when they come, they seem glad to be there. Where they are, God seems pleased to roll up and, together, we enter a kind of "going with the flow" beyond anything I had ever experienced.

Painfully, agonizingly, I was learning to adjust my whole way of being to theirs. Initially, I wondered about buying them watches, but then found myself loathing my own watch! And arriving on time was, of course, only the beginning. My dear friends would drift in and out of the meeting according to God's will, or to meet the need for a fag, or to respond to the needs of a tiny one. The way to sort out the pandemonium created by the little ones was - so I felt - to get more staff. How would any of the adults be able to complete my lovely course if their kids were not looked after and given appropriate teaching in another room? Staff came, staff went, unable to adjust. As I went flapping around the place trying to keep the show on the road, the Romany adults remained utterly untroubled and unaware that there was any problem. Perhaps it was I who was the problem and I who needed to change.

I remembered that, when our own three children had been born, I had been very irritated by the way everybody talked about a baby arriving "early" or "late". The date of birth had been calculated by science and was regarded as correct and therefore to be honoured by all. But, what about the poor baby? Was it not allowed to arrive when God was willing? Even before birth we were conditioning our offspring into our obsession with *chronos* time!

As a professional clarinettist, I had often lamented the fact that inspiration could not be switched on at will. It might come during the performance; it might even come - if you were very lucky - when the red recording light was on. But it could equally well come when you were busking in the bathroom. I had always felt that somewhere along the road our culture had taken a wrong turn. The most precious and edifying things in life could all too easily become a tyranny, if you tried to bottle them. So much of life, as I had come to know it, seemed grasp rather than gift, law rather than grace. And the only kind of spirit that you could successfully bottle was certainly not the Spirit who comes and goes as He pleases!

Gradually, as the weeks went by our new Romany Cluster began to develop a life and ethos of its own. Through trial and error I discovered what worked and what didn't and I came to recognize that I was on a far steeper learning curve than my new friends.

Chapter Ten

"Jesus was a Romany"

July 2008

Sharron, Pashey & Sophia

One of the great highlights of each year for me was our annual church camping trip to "Little Switzerland". Perched in the Folkestone cliffs, there was a marvellous view from the campsite over to France. We had built up good relations with the site's owner and were allowed to get on and be a church family together without having to worry too much about lots of rules and regulations. From Spring 2008 I had begun to invite some of the Romanies to come camping with the rest of us from the 11.15 service. Most of their parents' generation had known the nomadic life in a wagon and so they warmed to the idea of a camping trip. However, they had no kit and lots of children, so there were a number of practical difficulties to think through. Right up to the eleventh hour I was not sure whether God would be willing, not least since the weather forecast predicted torrential rain in the area for the whole weekend. In the end we decided to head off and go with the flow.

Two Romany families joined the rest of us from St Dunstan's and Roy set up an amazing barbecue under a gazebo and provided three communal barbecues over the weekend. For fuel we had packed a large quantity of oak logs from the Vicarage garden. There on the campsite, I saw a side of Roy that I had not seen before. He was completely in his element as outdoor chef catering for about forty of us. I, too, was in my element as one who has had a life long passion for camping and the outdoor life. Cultural differences between us seemed to melt away in the great outdoors and someone commented, "Jesus was a Romany".

Roy as chef

We explored this idea together but not in a joking or even a romantic way. Abraham, the father of all, had, after all, been "a wandering Aramean." Indeed, the Jews were formed into a nation in their own right during the time of their Exodus from slavery in Egypt. Over a period of forty years, they had moved together through the wilderness, guided by a pillar of cloud by day and a pillar of fire by night, and pitching their tents wherever God directed. Like the Romanies, they were travellers. The nomadic life was in their blood. Moving on to the New Testament, John's Gospel has something remarkably similar to say about Jesus. He is the word made flesh, who came down to earth and "pitched his tent" among his own people.[15] He was the one who said of himself that, whilst foxes might have holes and birds might have nests, the Son of Man had nowhere to lay his head. Jesus was a traveller, one constantly on the move. Our Romany friends lamented the loss of their nomadic existence and would often say how hard they found it to be "bricked up" in houses.

Out there on the campsite there was not a cloud in the sky. The predictions of the metreologists proved wildly wrong and the sun shone on us the whole weekend. Nature was having its own way and God was having his own way with us, too. We had escaped, if only for a few days, from the tyranny of a mechanistic way of life governed by cold reason. Was this a glimpse of what Jesus called "life in all its fullness"?

Our practice, over the years, had been to hold the Sunday morning service on an old WWII bunker at the top of the cliffs. The view into Folkestone, down into the campsite and over to France had always been inspiring. However, this year, we tried something new. Roy had

---

[15] John 1:14 και ο λογος σαρξ εγενετο και εσκηνωσεν εν ημιν
"And the Word (Christ) became flesh (human, incarnate) and tabernacled (fixed His tent of flesh, lived awhile) among us" (Amplified Bible)

expressed to me privately a deep longing to be baptised again by full immersion. I explained that we believed in one baptism and that he had already had that. However, we would be able to have a re-affirmation of baptism for him if that was his heart's desire. I then suggested that this might take place in the English Channel at the camping weekend. Roy seemed delighted at the idea and asked if his little Derby might also be baptised on the occasion. Once ten-year old little Roy got wind of the plans he also asked for re-affirmation by full immersion. And so, that year of 2008, we all headed off to the beach for our Sunday morning service with a few extras travelling over from Cranbrook to join us. There was an extraordinary sense of freedom and joy as we sang, broke open the scriptures and waded out into the sea. The life-death drama of baptism in the sea was made all the more real by the fact that neither big Roy nor little Roy can swim. Alan (one of our authorized lay ministers at St Dunstan's) and I shared the awesome responsibility of walking them out into the "deep waters of death", recalling both how Moses had led his people from captivity into freedom as they passed through the Red Sea and how Jesus had descended into hell itself before rising to resurrection life on the third day.

Roy is baptised into Christ – Alan & Martin [16]

Back on the beach, I reminded the worshippers how, in the year 597,

---

[16] Photo copyright of Dennis Coburn

Augustine and his wee band of monks had rowed up on Kentish shores just a few miles east of Folkestone, bringing the Roman expression of the Christian faith into our land. But, within my own heart, I pondered whether our wild outdoor gathering was closer to the spirit of the New Testament church than the highly regimented, top-heavy faith of Rome that has controlled most of our gatherings for the last 1,400 years. Just for an hour, on that Folkestone beach, we were able to taste another way of being church together, another way of worshipping. Salt water, sand, sun and wind stung our flesh. Our spirits sang. Jesus showed up.

Chapter Eleven

Archi-diaconal Orders

Many an Episcopal eyebrow may have been raised on reading this account of baptism in the sea. Can a sacrament ordained by the Lord himself be conducted on ground that has not been consecrated? Had the local vicar's permission been sought and granted for this ceremony? And what about the water? Can one bless the waters of the entire English Channel?

Some years earlier, I had felt it important to speak to the Archdeacon about another similar question. I explained to him that, whenever I used the authorised canonical words of the liturgy at baptism, I felt that the people went to sleep on me. Their eyes would be glued to the words of the card they were given to hold as, anxiously, they would wait for the next bit printed in bold type indicating when they were to join in, often only to be told that their response had been too half-hearted. Moreover, I was only too conscious that, at these ceremonies, the language we used required both a certain level of literacy and of theological understanding. And, even for the highly educated, the recitation of printed liturgy seemed to have the effect of creating a kind of critical distance between the divine mysteries and the worshippers. I felt God himself was being kept at arms length, as we slavishly reproduced words drawn up by a liturgical committee. I felt that the Archdeacon was with me as I shared these thoughts with him. So I plucked up courage and requested permission to put the liturgy to one side at my next baptism, so that I would be set free to explain what was going on in my own words. I shall never forget his answer:

"I order you to do this!"

Looking back, I believe that these orders marked a significant change in my whole approach to bringing people into the presence of God. I was not just being given permission to do things in culturally relevant ways, adapting my style to the people and the occasion. I was being ordered to do this.

The new 11.15 Sunday service that we started in 2002 marked the real beginning of my journey into the unknown and my determination to try to be relevant and real with people. It was simply not good enough to say that God's grace comes to bear on the lives of those at the receiving end of sacramental ministry, irrespective of whether they have a clue of what is going on or not. However true this may be for the baptised baby or mentally handicapped adult, it should never be an excuse for hiding behind words written by teams of scholars, however holy and inspired they may be. Never is this truer than when bringing the grace of God to a community of people who, for the most part, are illiterate. I came to believe that, if ever there was a group of people who needed a fresh approach, it was the Romanies.

The chapters that now follow tell the story of the marvellous outpouring of God's grace on a people truly hungry for his blessing. I am now convinced that if the Archdeacon has said "no" on the day I went to see him and I had had to continue reading the long liturgy at every baptism, then what God was clearly up to would have been snuffed out overnight. However, I was being encouraged in other ways to press on with my new informal, creative approach. For, in the Anglican Church, there is now a growing passion and openness to doing things in fresh ways when circumstances dictate. Since Augustine had arrived on Kentish shores all those centuries ago, we had been trapped within an ecclesiology that threatened to keep God in a kind of cultural time warp. For fourteen hundred years it had been assumed that what worked in one place and in one generation had to be right for every place and every generation. Now, at last, from Archbishop Rowan Williams down, we were being actively encouraged to bring the Gospel to bear on the lives of people where they where and not where the institution though they should be. Hallelujah!

Chapter Twelve

Vicarage Oak

Before unfolding the remarkable events of 2008, I need to first go back to the year of 2007 and tell the story behind the vicarage oak which we had used to fuel our BBQ at the church camping weekend. The year 2007 had begun with the falling of one of the massive, two hundred year-old oaks that had been planted on either side of the vicarage drive. One Thursday, I had been asleep in the afternoon on my day off whilst gale force winds were sweeping across the land. On waking, I picked up the phone to discover that the line was dead. I wondered if the winds had blown down the telephone cable and went outside to have a look. The oak tree to the left of the drive had simply disappeared! It had been uprooted by the force of the wind and had fallen - just missing vicarage and sleeping vicar - completely flattening our garage and taking the telephone cable with it. In Old Testament times this would have been understood as an act of God.

For many months we tried to work out what to do with the huge, five-ton trunk that lay outside the vicarage. At the point when Margareta and I were beginning to despair of what to do, a burly man arrived at the vicarage and introduced himself as "Frank".

Frank offered to deal with the massive trunk, stump and roots. After a lot of wheeling and dealing, we agreed that he would take on the job. As the work went on, I gradually got to know Frank and his family. Sometimes, they would arrive at the vicarage together with strong male relatives and a large supporting cast of wives and children. Senior patriarchs from the dynasty would also come along to offer their counsel. As time went on, I enjoyed entering into their world and observing how decisions were made and how the name of the good Lord was invariably invoked whenever the task seemed humanly impossible. The challenge took on an epic quality with ever-larger chain saws, cranes and vehicles being brought in to deal with the tons of oak. However, the greatest challenge to Frank and his team came right at the end, when they attempted to move the huge oak chairs they had crafted from the front of the garden to the back. This took every male available plus a truck. The final placing of the oak chairs in a ring brought the men to their knees in more ways than one.

To celebrate the completion of the job, I brought out a big tray of tea and cake for all. Finally I discovered that Frank was, in fact, the brother of Roy and Moses. Furthermore, Frank's wife Naomi was Rachel's sister. Patriarch Levi and matriarch Charlotte were parents to the women folk and I began to understand more fully just how closely interwoven all the families were. Within any large dynasty of people there is, of course, a whole history of joys and sorrows, of love and of broken relationships. As these passionate people opened out their lives to me on the vicarage lawn that day, I sensed that God was going to do something remarkable within their number in the days to come. Their openness gave me permission to be open with them. I challenged them to let go of whatever might need letting go of and to find a new way forward under God. I realized I was taking a big risk in being so bold and putting them on the spot in this way, and I felt very vulnerable and somewhat wimpish next this great clan of travellers. But, in another way, I felt I really had nothing to lose. I had tried, for many years, to speak into the lives of people from my own culture and had never really felt that I had broken the ice. Curiously, I realized that I felt safer with this 'bunch of gypsies' than I did with some of my own people. It crossed my mind that Jesus had come to his own, but his own had not received him.[17] I also remembered how St Paul had had little success with his own people, only breaking through with the gentiles.

Now, here I was, standing before a group of people with whom I had almost nothing in common, finding that we were taking each other very seriously. We were, for each other, what the Gospels call "people of peace," people who were open to hearing from each other, people with whom the values of the Kingdom of God could take root. As we chatted together, there in the sun in the back garden of the vicarage, Martin became all emotionable again, just as he had done at Roy's wedding a few years earlier. One or two of the adults became emotionable too - tough men standing, wet-eyed, alongside their vicar as he led them

---

[17] John 1:11

in prayer. I felt I had broken open for them a hitherto unarticulated longing for deep reconciliation and peace. Without knowing it, they were searching for a new way forward and it had taken a complete outsider to show them the first steps. In days to come, some of them would become "oaks of righteousness".

Chapter thirteen

"Blessed are those who mourn"

By summer 2008 our Friday Romany cluster that met at Church House was reasonably well established and I was getting to know quite a few others from the broader Romany network that extended right across East Sussex and Kent. Although Pastor Lywood's ministry with them had come to an end some twenty-five years earlier, the phrase "converted and baptised" continued to represent the first two critical steps in becoming a follower of Jesus. A number of the Romanies began to share with me their desire to be baptised, and it seemed very important to them that they had checked out and approved the person they wanted to do this for them. This process of assessment took place within each of the families and it became clear to me that long and careful discussions were going on, led by the senior patriarch in the family. Once a common view was reached the family would adopt this as a whole and begin to share it with other relatives in the broader network. In my culture we would call it 360-degree appraisal. The decision to go for baptism was thus made collectively, in the same way that was clearly the case in the New Testament church. Just as the Philippian jailer's whole household was baptised by Paul following the extraordinary events of the night, so Moses was leading his whole family forward for baptism.[18] It was far more important to them that they would present themselves as a complete family unit, than that any individual foibles and misgivings be entertained. Indeed, each family member, who was old enough to have developed a personal view, clearly put the collective decision before everything else. The unspoken assumption was this: "If we are going to be baptised, then it will be all of us together or not at all!"

The incident reminded me of a book I had been captivated by back in 1980, when still working as a musician in Glasgow. Vincent Donovan, an American missionary, had brought the Gospel to the Masai tribes of Tanzania, a story he captured in his book 'An Epistle from the Masai'.

---

[18] Acts 16:33-34

I recalled in particular the moment when the local leader of one clan put the missionary on the spot, challenging his whole outlook towards conversion and baptism.

"The old man, Ndangoya, stopped me politely but firmly, "Padre, why are you trying to break us up and separate us? During this whole year that you have been teaching us, we have talked about these things when you were not here, at night around the fire. Yes, there have been lazy ones in this community. But, they have been helped by those with much energy. There are stupid ones in the community, but they have been helped by those who are intelligent. Yes, there are ones with little faith in this village, but they have been helped by those with much faith. Would you turn out and drive off the lazy ones and the ones with little faith and the stupid ones? From the first day I have spoken for these people. And I speak for them now. Now, on this day one year later, I can declare for them and for all this community, that we have reached the step in our lives where we can say, 'We believe.'" [19]

I found this same communal way of functioning amidst the Romanies hugely compelling, for here was a people who had already encoded, within their collective DNA, the deep desire to "keep the unity of the Spirit through the bond of peace".[20] Here was a people who had not been touched by the individualism that has cursed my own culture for the last four hundred years. Here was a people who could say of themselves, "We belong, therefore we are!"

I became most deeply aware of this when I observed how the Romanies dealt with bereavement. That summer of 2008 saw the death of one of their great patriarchs, Aaron, father of Roy, Moses, Frank and three other sons and three daughters; father of nine and grandfather of about forty. To my great sadness, I was out of the country when Aaron died. When I returned, toward the end of August, I heard the news of Aaron's death and was told that his burial had already taken place a few days

[19] Vincent Donovan – Christianity Rediscovered, *An Epistle from the Masai* 1978 page 92
[20] Ephesians 4:3

40

earlier. I was devastated that I had not been there for them in their hour of need. As I went around to visit, I was profoundly struck by the way deep grief had swept through their whole community like a huge tidal wave of sorrow. Everyone was in mourning right across the generations. Grief was, to these Romanies, not a private matter; it was, of its very nature, communal. The very air of each home seemed to grieve. Time stood still. There was no sense whatever of life having to get going again as quickly as possible. I felt deeply convicted. When my own father had died a few years earlier, I had reacted by losing myself in a frenzy of work, in a hopeless attempt to deal with my grief by keeping my mind active.

Before setting off on holiday that summer of 2008 we had provisionally planned Sunday 31 August as the day when Moses and his family would be baptised. On hearing the news of his father's death, I wondered whether the family would wish to wait till a later date for the baptisms. However, as I began to share in their grief, it became very clear that the Lord had been active in their hearts all through the month during which I had been away. The experience of bereavement had, clearly, brought them all much closer to God and they seemed hungry to go deeper. I remembered how those Jesus calls "blessed," are not necessarily the ones riding along on the crest of the wave. Rather, it is those who mourn who are the blessed, and it is they who Jesus says will receive comfort. [21] From within the depths of their shared grief, a desire arose to go ahead with the planned baptism although it would only be a week or so away. Together, we made sense of events by remembering how to be baptised is to enter into the very death and resurrection of Jesus himself. Aaron had died and he would rise with Jesus. Those who were to be baptised would walk the same path, even within this earthly life.

Paul put this so beautifully in his letter to the Philippians. Who knows, maybe he shared these words with the jailer of the town of Philippi, as he and his family were baptised into Christ:

"I want to know Christ
yes, to know the power of his resurrection and participation in his
sufferings,
becoming like him in his death, and so, somehow,

---

[21] Matthew 5:4

attaining to the resurrection from the dead."[22]

And so, plans for the Cranbrook baptisms went ahead. Moses and his clan were to be baptised and, as they shared with other relatives who arrived at their home, so Lottie, Rachel's sister, decided that she and her four children would also be baptised, as would Iris and her two children. For some time another couple, Stephen and Danielle, had also been thinking about baptism as a prelude to getting married in the following year. They had found the camping trip quite transformative and were all ready to go. I rushed around to Cranbrook School to confirm that their lovely open-air swimming pool was still available for the forthcoming Sunday, only to discover that it was just about to be emptied for the winter. I had made my booking just in time.

---

[22] Philippians 3:10-11

Chapter fourteen

From Death to Life

31 August 2008

"Open now the crystal fountain,
Whence the healing stream doth flow;
Let the fire and cloudy pillar
Lead me all my journey through.
Strong Deliverer, strong Deliverer,
Be Thou still my Strength and Shield;
Be Thou still my Strength and Shield.

When I tread the verge of Jordan,
Bid my anxious fears subside;
Death of deaths, and hell's destruction,
Land me safe on Canaan's side.
Songs of praises, songs of praises,
I will ever give to Thee;
I will ever give to Thee." [23]

---

[23] "Guide me O thou great redeemer". Words: William Williams; Music: John Hughes

The baptism of seventeen people hardly compares with the three thousand who were baptised by the Apostles on the day of Pentecost. However, for a small, traditional market town like Cranbrook, this was something quite unusual. Baptism by full immersion had probably no precedent at St Dunstan's, other than the single occasion in 1710 when the local vicar, Revd John Johnston, had baptised a candidate in this way. To this day, people continue to come to see the bizarre full immersion font he had constructed just inside the south door. It is not surprising that the font was only used once, for the candidate had to walk down into the narrow, nine-feet-deep concrete chamber. It must have been a terrifying experience and a lot of fun and games to fill it up with water. We are told that the reason he had the font built was to be able to compete with the local Baptists who, at that time, were baptising many adult converts by full immersion.

The Romany adults usually wanted full immersion baptism principally because this was how John the Baptist had baptised Jesus in the river Jordan. What Jesus had, they wanted. He had set the pattern, they believed, that adults should follow. Perhaps in the back of their mind was also the memory of how Pastor Lywood had done it. I myself had recently read the *Didache,* which confirmed that, in the early church of the first century, full immersion baptism was regarded as best practice whenever it was possible. The memory of the baptisms in the sea earlier that summer, were also fresh in our memory.

The regulars at our Sunday 11.15 service had been used to innovative ways of worshipping since the service was started in 2002. And so, on the 31st of August 2008, having completed the first part of the service, it felt quite natural to lead the congregation out of church and along to the school swimming pool. The Romanies had no background in formal church worship and so they joined in with the outdoor ceremony as though this were the most normal thing to do. For them it is entirely in order to be at once completely laid back and deeply committed. Informality does not have to be equated with shallow spirituality. The free spirits of the Romanies helped the rest of us to relax, let go of our anxieties about propriety and enter into the wonder of what has happening at an unseen, spiritual level.

Moses baptised into Christ [24]

Each and every one of the seventeen candidates that day received the unconditional and unearned grace of God in baptism and this narrative will continue to explore the way in which so many of our lives have been transformed during these days. But I want to single out just one person. I had never in my fifty-six years of life and fourteen years of ordained ministry seen anyone so dramatically transformed, as was Moses that day. He entered the cold water of the pool one man. He

[24] Photo copyright of Dennis Coburn

stepped out another. The "old Adam" had been withdrawn and sullen, morose and lacking self-confidence. The "new Adam" simply shone from the moment his face emerged from the water. In an instant he was born again. The old had gone; the new had come. It was as though the water had washed away everything that was not of God and the sparkling light of the bright sun was bathing him in the Holy Spirit, empowering him to become all that God had created him to be. Until that day I had come to believe that the grace of God made available in the sacrament would unfold in hidden and mysterious ways over the life of the person, that the action of the water was essentially symbolic and metaphorical. But on that day I saw, for the first time, that spiritual transformation may be as instantaneous and dramatic as the birth of a baby into the world.

Moses in Deal, March 2009

Since Moses' baptism many of his closest relatives have commented to me on what has happened to him. One young Romany girl told me that visiting Moses' home had overnight become an entirely new experience. His home then quickly became a centre of light, a place to which people were drawn, like moths to a flame. I wondered whether the Philippian Jailor's home had been changed in this way following his baptism and whether Lydia, the women who traded in purple cloth in the same city, had opened her home to others following her baptism.

The Lord had guided our Moses through the wilderness, through the deep waters of death and now, praise God, he had landed him safe on Canaan's side. Behind him followed a whole community of travellers, hoping against hope that, ahead of them, there beckoned a land flowing with milk and honey, a land of freedom and hope. We were just beginning to glimpse what God was saying to us through the burning bush, that Moses' daughter, Charlotte, had seen earlier that year!

Moses' spiritual re-birth led me to ask why such transformations are not commonplace. Was it simply, as little Roy had said, that these were special times, and that "God had drawn near"? Were such outpourings of his grace random and unusual and, therefore, not to be expected? But again I wondered whether God had found it easy to draw near to the Romanies precisely because their world-view was holistic and open, free from cynicism and scepticism. They were open to feeling the movement of the Holy Spirit in the very action of cold water and bright sunshine.

A growing desire arose in my own heart to be re-born, to be landed safe on Canaan's side, to be delivered from the dualistic world that my education had instilled in me. These Romanies were my teachers; I was their disciple. If our brother Moses could be changed like this, in the twinkling of an eye, then maybe there was hope for all of us.

"For I will take you out of the nations;
I will gather you from all the countries and bring you back to your own land.
I will sprinkle clean water on you and you will be clean;
I will cleanse you from all your impurities and from all your idols.
I will give you a new heart and put a new spirit in you;
I will remove from you your heart of stone and give you a heart of flesh…
… then you will live in the land I gave your ancestors;
you will be my people and I will be your God."[25]

---

[25] Ezekiel 36:24-28

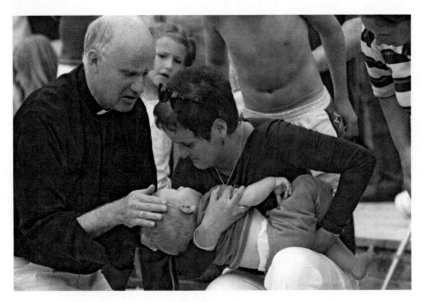

Levi baptised into Christ - Martin & Margareta [26]

Chapter fifteen

"I have called you by name, and you are mine!"
10 September 2008

Close on the heels of these baptisms came the possibility of confirmation for the adults. By a stroke of good fortune, Bishop Stephen would be holding a service just a fortnight later down the road in Marden parish church. Quickly, names were submitted to the Bishop and the trip planned. Some years earlier, Roy and Pashey had been confirmed in the Cathedral, now they were to be followed by Roy's brother, Moses, together with Rachel, Charlotte, Annie, Lottie, Stephen and Danielle, as well as another non-Romany from our church. I explained to them all, how it had been the practice since the days of the early church for the Bishop of the area to place his hands on the head of those who had just been baptised, confirming them and praying especially for more of the Holy Spirit.

The whole outing to Marden had a great sense of fun about it. Smaller members of Romany families usually come along on such occasions too. I positioned myself on the end of a pew as near as possible to my candidates to keep an eye on them since they had hardly ever attended a long formal service where they would need to know what to do and say at certain points. I had explained to them that, early on in the service, I would be required to stand and introduce each of them by name to the congregation. Each of them would then stand, bow to the Bishop, and turn to face the people. When it came to this solemn moment I looked over and observed that most of my people were no longer there!

I nipped across the aisle and was told that nature had summoned them and that they had hastened out of church to meet their need. Somewhat inelegantly I explained this to the congregation, reminded myself that even King David's need had got a mention in scripture, and began to pray that the faithful departed would manage to make it back into church for the next thing they needed to do in the ceremony. They crept in the door just at the moment when all the candidates had

49

been invited by the Bishop to gather round the font to dip their finger in the water, make the sign of the cross of their forehead and remind themselves that Jesus had died for their sins on the cross. It was only after the service that I discovered that the good Lord had come to the rescue of my friends, and provided a nearby bush for them. From then on we were simply going with the flow!

At the end of the service, Bishop Stephen led all the candidates out into the porch and prayed with them. Several of my people told me how at that point they had felt the surge of the Holy Spirit sweep through their body. I loved the way my Romany friends were able to move from the ridiculous straight to the sublime without any sense of anything being out of place or inappropriate. The Bishop commented to me, "they're full of it, aren't they!" God was there, he was all in all, he was Lord of all their needs from the most basic to the most holy. Immanence and transcendence meet and kiss in these dear people. Meanwhile, we continue to argue about whether or not toilets should be provided in church!

The occasion is memorable in one other way too. Bishop Stephen had said, at the beginning of the ceremony, that the candidates should not be surprised if they received God's blessing in special ways following the confirmation. Two things happened a little later that I subsequently reported to the Bishop. One of the candidates, Stephen, discovered to his delight and amazement that he was to become a father. He had given up all hope that he and Danielle would conceive, since he had been told by doctors years earlier, following a kick in the groin by a horse, that he would remain infertile for the rest of his life.

The second blessing came one evening during a Friday cluster meeting. Lottie explained to us that she had just learned that her son, Mark, would have to have a major operation on one of his eyes. We prayed hard for him there and then.

Two days later, on Sunday, Lottie told us - and Mark confirmed – how, at the very moment when we had prayed, Mark had experienced a sudden clearing of his vision during a football game he was taking part in up the road at the sports centre. He had been about to give up the game, such was the blurring in his eyesight.

Some months later, it became clear that the operation would still be needed and, in the final chapter of this book, I will recall the day this happened. We walk by faith, not by sight.

Chapter sixteen

"God chose the lowly things."

Throughout this period I found myself operating on two radically different planes as I carried my duties as vicar of Cranbrook. Whilst my duties as steward of the church fabric had left me embroiled in serious political wrangling in the parish, I found myself at the same time in a state of awe and wonder at the blessings God was pouring out on this small, discrete and marginalized part of the community. I was at a loss how to deal with the former and was simply being swept along by what I perceived God to be doing in the latter. The contrast between these two parallel universes could not have been starker and more perplexing.

"Praise be to the Lord,
for he showed me the wonders of his love
when I was in a city under siege." [27]

One sleepless night, pondering these things, I came up with a formula, which seemed to make sense to me. The politically strong appeared to be spiritually weak, whilst the politically weak appeared spiritually strong. I became aware of strong biblical resonances to support this way of seeing things. Writing to the Corinthian church, Paul wrote:

"Brothers and sisters, think of what you were when you were called.
Not many of you were wise by human standards;
not many were influential; not many were of noble birth.
But God chose the foolish things of the world to shame the wise;
God chose the weak things of the world to shame the strong.
God chose the lowly things of the world
and the despised things - and the things that are not-
to nullify the things that are,
so that no-one may boast before him." [28]

---

[27] Psalm 31:21
[28] 1 Corinthians 1:26-29

Charlotte, Zaman, Barbara, Haroon & Pashey- just baptised into Christ

Similarly, towards the end of his life, Paul had come to discover at a personal level, that God's grace was most apparent to him when he was at his wits' end. "I delight in weaknesses, in insults, in hardships, in persecutions, in difficulties. For when I am weak, then I am strong!"[29] The very difficulties we were going through, as a parish church, were having the effect of bringing the Gospel into ever-sharper focus for me. The values of this world were all turned upside down by the values of the Gospel. However, the institution of the church was constantly in danger of selling out to the values of this world. This became apparent in the way people responded to events in the parish.

I was delighted when the local press agreed to print the group photo of the seventeen who had been baptised on 31 August. At last some of the good news coming from the local parish church would be shared with the broader community. Most of the bad news coming from our church had found its way straight onto the front page, with bill-boards outside the newsagents on both sides of the high street re-enforcing the story.

---

[29] 2 Corinthians 12:10

The photo of the seventeen baptisms was however, placed deep inside the papers. In one paper it was coupled with some bad news about our current financial crisis. Side by side in this paper was the great news of an awakening of faith in the local Romany community and the story about the church's lack of cash. At that time I also began to print out the photos of each of the baptisms on A3 paper and display them in the church porch.

As I monitored how people were affected by the news of their local parish church, certain patterns began to emerge. There was much discussion about money and all manner of explanations were being offered as to why we had the crisis and what should be done about it. But there was a virtual silence on the subject of the Romany awakening of faith. It seemed significant to me that these two areas of *stewardship* and of *mission* were both central themes in the early chapters of the book of Acts. I was fascinated that the newspaper had (perhaps unwittingly) brought them together.

I took the newspaper article along to a meeting of some of the most senior people in the Diocese and passed it around at the beginning of the meeting for all to see. I was profoundly shocked by the response of those present. The article prompted a long and detailed discussion relating to finance. It was an important, indeed vital, discussion to have taken place. But at no point in the whole meeting was the awakening of faith amongst the Romanies ever mentioned. I felt no anger about this at all; I simply felt deep dismay that the very best brains and talent in our church's leadership had become so preoccupied with management issues as to have become blind to seeing what God was doing. Had the church become so preoccupied with money that there was simply no room left on our agendas for mission? The whole sweep of the New Testament places mission before everything else. But we have turned this on its head. We have placed internal good housekeeping at the top, and placed mission, especially mission to the poor and the marginalized, as an optional extra at the bottom. As a church, we had forsaken our birthright.

Is the parish priest to be first and foremost an administrator, or an apostle? This question had become ever more urgent and pressing for me. Over my years in Cranbrook, I had come to distance myself ever more intentionally, from the inherited pressure on me to be a kind of chaplain to the prevailing culture. I was more interested, you might say, in baptizing people, than in baptizing the status quo. Turning aside to focus on mission, however, was understood by many to be a dereliction of duty. But by now, the call to mission had become irresistible.

Later in October 2008 a word was given to us from a group of German pastors with whom Margareta and I were on retreat in Tuscany:

> "These are the words of him who is holy and true,
> who holds the key of David.
> What he opens no-one can shut,
> and what he shuts no-one can open.
> I have placed before you an open door that no-one can shut.
> I know that you have little strength,
> Yet you have kept my word and have not denied my name".[30]

---

[30] Revelation 3:7-8

Chapter Seventeen

"Sing a new song"[31]

We played the pipe and you sang!
We played the pipe and you danced![32]

Meanwhile, back in our growing Romany Cluster I was discovering new things every week. In so many ways my new friends knew so much more about community than I. Most of my formative years I had spent practising the clarinet for many hours a day alone in a room. As a theological student and as a curate I had carried over the same dedication to study and further personal development. Whilst this had borne some fruit and had secured me a living, I was beginning to understand that there were vital areas of human development that had passed me by.

Mainstream British culture values education very highly: we view a lack of systematic education as a curse and reserve our highest praise

---

[31] Psalm 98 "Sing to the Lord a new song, for he has done new things; his right hand and his holy arm have worked salvation for him."
[32] Jesus said: 'We played the flute for you, and you did not dance; we sang a dirge and you did not mourn.' Matthew 11.17

for those whose formal educational achievement is greatest. Any school speech day bears testimony to this. The Romanies had been denied any hope of the kind of elitist education I had enjoyed but they possess a kind of intelligence that we know little of. I would like to call it "community intelligence".

Over time, I discovered that there are, for them, two vital elements in community life. The first is song and dance, the second is eating together. In 2002, just as we were beginning the new 11.15 Sunday service, I had taught the congregation a very simple, unaccompanied song:

> "He came down that we might have joy .... [x3] ... hallelujah, for ever more.
>
> He came down that we might have peace...[x3] ... hallelujah, for ever more.
>
> He came down that we might have love.. [x3] ... hallelujah, for ever more."

I have a very poor natural singing voice and, back then, it seemed clear that it would not help to have the vicar teaching new songs in this way and my own highly musical family wisely cautioned me not to persist with this. However, now, some six years later, I plucked up the courage to try it once more in the new setting of the Romany Cluster. I started to sing the same song again. To my great joy and amazement Roy, Pashey and little Roy started singing along with me as though we had learnt it only yesterday and as though there were no tomorrow. The rest of their sons instantly picked it up along with all the others there. Within a few minutes, about twenty of us were all singing our hearts out. I was amazed by their total lack of inhibition and embarrassment - they sang loud and gustily.

In that moment, I finally let go of any lingering musical perfectionism that still needed programming out of me and gave in to the Spirit. For I felt the Spirit's presence, powerfully building unseen bonds between us. When hearts and minds are united together in this way, real mutual listening takes place and, however rough and ready the result may be, the total is always greater than the sum of the parts. Community is born of song.

We needed to be mindful that most of our adults over thirty were illiterate and not a few others could only just read. With this in mind, I began to add new songs week by week to our repertoire. By spring 2009 we had fifteen that could be struck up at a moment's notice. Our signature song quickly became

"Give me joy in my heart, keep me burning!
Give me love in my heart …
Give me joy in my heart …"

Lottie, Charlotte, Annie, Rachel, Pashey

More and more I experienced the absence of word sheets or books as liberation rather than limitation. The theology of our songs does not and cannot draw on the rich quarry that the educated enjoy. However, singing words you have learned by heart opens out all kinds of possibilities denied to those who need words in print or on screen; suddenly it becomes possible to sing driving down the road, under the shower, in each other's homes, or at the beach. Simplicity of words does not have to mean a dumbing-down of the faith to raw basics.

After all, Karl Barth, when asked what the message of the Bible was for him, did not point to all the many theological books he had written. He simply responded: Jesus loves me. I know it because the Bible tells me so. When we sing, each person is free to understand words like love, joy or peace at their own level. As I shall explore later, towards the end of this book, a naïve faith is not necessarily a shallow faith. Those in their first joy need those who have been disciples for longer. Those who are mature in their faith absolutely need those who are still in their first joy! Young Charlene, just fifteen, phoned me once to thank me for the meeting of the previous night. I asked her what she had found most special. She said it was big Mark being there and joining in. "Yes, Martin, I think the singing went through him."

After a little time, Revd Ben Bentham, chaplain of Bethany School, started to show an interest in the Romany Cluster. He began to teach us new songs, which were quickly assimilated into the life stream of the community. The sheer simplicity of these songs makes them accessible across all generations and can be readily adapted to the needs of the moment. One new song Ben taught us goes like this:

> "In this place, Lord, be glorified, be glorified,
> In this place, Lord, be glorified today."

When we come to prayer ministry, we lay hands on each person and all sing for that person: "In Aaron's life, Lord, be glorified, be glorified…" I encourage those who are especially close to Aaron, to draw near. If the person we are praying for is not there, sometimes someone else can receive the prayer on their behalf. This can happen quite naturally. It was especially poignant, for example, when little Roy received prayer on behalf of his father, big Roy.

I sometimes reminded them how Mary sang "My soul *magnifies* the Lord," when the Angel Gabriel informed her that she would bear a son, who would be called Jesus. Following this pattern, we sing together, "In Rachel's life, Lord, be *magnified…*" We then move on to gathering up all the fragments of all our lives, singing "In *our lives*, Lord, be *magnified…*" This helps keep everyone focused and involved in the prayer. I have also discovered, that these words are lovely to sing over someone who is sick, for it demands nothing of the Lord other than that He be glorified/magnified in that persons' life. The outcome of the prayer for healing is thus left with Him. He will be glorified whether in sickness or in health. Together in song, we rejoice with those who are on the crest of the wave and we feel the pain of those who are suffering. This kind of communal prayer cannot be achieved easily with speech. For, in song, the pace is wonderfully stretched out and all the voices melt into each other and into a higher synthesis. As St Augustine famously said, "to sing is to pray twice!"

Levi & Kelly-Rose

The freedom from the printed word also sets us free in another very important way. My wife, Margareta, has developed this to a high level; indeed it has been in many ways her life's work. For years, I have stood on the edge, marvelling at how she gets people first to sing, and then to move. Occasionally, she reverses this, getting people to move to a rhythm and then introducing a song to accompany the movement. In 2007, helped greatly by Sue and Phil Crocker who offered to take on the administration, she formed a local community choir in

Cranbrook. It became known as *TiDo*. Before long, over forty of us were learning new songs and getting our bodies to move to the rhythm. My apprenticeship in *TiDo* [33] was providing me with a few basic skills and, above all, the necessary nerve to get people singing and moving without anything in their hands. Whilst *TiDo* only attracts individuals from my own culture who are able to cope with this kind of thing, within the Romany Community I have yet to meet anyone who is not at ease with singing and moving. Indeed, the moment I had the courage to have a go, I discovered that they had been patiently waiting for the singing and dancing to get going for some time.

Every year at the local Primary School there is a Romany gathering to which everyone is invited. In 2007 I knew only a few of those present. A year later, I know nearly all of them and am able to join in the song and dance. Never, not even for a moment, was I ever made to feel that I was encroaching on their cultural territory and pretending to be someone I wasn't. In a very deep sense, it felt as though they had adopted me. "Your kind, Martin, we call *gorgios*." To be a *gorgia* means simply to be a non-Romany. There do not seem to be any negative overtones to being a *gorgia*. Indeed, they don't seem to have the kind of pejorative words for us that we have for them like "gypsy" and "pikey". So I found I was able to move in and out of the two cultures quite freely. The two Romany earrings on the cover of this book symbolize the two cultures. A little later, I will be exploring more fully the overlap and cultural interface between the two.

---

[33] As in Do Re, Me Fa … *TiDo*

Chapter eighteen

"Eat, drink and be merry, for tomorrow we die!"

Lottie & Pashey

Song and dance are key elements in the building of community life but far more important still is the discipline of eating together. In the early days of getting to know the Romanies I noticed that, whenever I popped round to their homes, I would invariably be handed a cup of tea shortly after arriving. After some time, this hospitality went to the next stage and I would be presented with something to eat. I was always glad of the food but did not realize the deeper message for some time. To be offered food and drink was their way of feeding me the message that they accepted me and welcomed me as one of the extended family. To have rejected the offer, would have been tantamount to rejecting the hand of friendship; unwittingly I had eaten my way into a new community!

In the early days of the new 11.15 Sunday service, Roy began to arrive at Church House with a large pot of soup he had made at home. There are a variety of different Romany soups. My favourite is the famous "Joy Grey". Quickly, I seized the opportunity and we ordered a soup urn to keep it warm on arrival. After the service we would walk over the churchyard to Church House to enjoy a communal lunch. Generally, one never knew when a soup might appear and so there was something wonderfully impromptu about the lunches. Roy might even disappear during a service to go and make a soup if he felt so moved. I began to realize that, for the Romanies, a gathering without food was not really a proper gathering. Since it was all but impossible for them to meet together in large numbers to eat, here was the church providing them with a way in which to form the very community they had lost when they had given up the nomadic way of life. The soup lunches proved to be a great way to get to know people better in an ultra laid-back setting. However, it became clear, after a while, that Romany style "table fellowship" was way out of the comfort zones of many of our regular *gorgios*[34] from the 11.15 community. In fact, as I only discovered after many months, Romanies don't really like to eat around a table, preferring to have their food on their lap while sitting, often on the floor. Romany living rooms don't even have tables for eating around, the space being kept open and free so that as many people as possible can come and go. Meanwhile, our middle class *gorgia* families, who were working hard at inculcating conventional table manners in their children, were, perhaps, reluctant to have their tiny ones mix with the Romany children who were, for the most part, allowed much greater freedom to do their own thing and roam free.

We had then something of a "Corinthian" problem on our hands. I tried to imagine what St. Paul might have written if he had had the task of bringing together different cultures and trying to make it work for all. In a later chapter, I will explore how these cultural differences impacted our sharing of the Lord's Supper.

After the urn, the next thing we introduced were some lovely big round tables, which could be very quickly put in place and on which we could place the food. There is one important formality, however, that they

---

[34] A non-Romany

always honour. The leader of the community is always fed first and seems to get the lion's share!

I came to love these shared meals and my heart would always leap when Roy or Moses would appear half way through the service in church and announce that a soup was on its way. The Romanies have a middle-eastern understanding of the sacramental nature of communal eating. To eat together is a profound outward sign of an unseen spiritual reality. The link with middle-eastern culture is not entirely surprising, since the Romanies are an ethnic group who, for some unknown reason, had to leave their homeland in northern India about a thousand years ago. The visual similarities are not difficult to see, and it is said that some Romany words have their roots in Hindi. Over the centuries they gradually dispersed westward, throughout Europe and, today, are most numerous in Eastern Europe and Russia.

One of the fascinating consequences of these lunches was that our little fellowship began to take on, more and more, the character of the New Testament church. For here was a place where anyone was welcome, irrespective of class, level of education or social standing. Waifs and strays of all kinds - vulnerable people who had nowhere else that they could call family - found a home within this wild multi-cultural gathering. The unemployed, single parents, adults with significant learning difficulties, asylum seekers and casual visitors all found a place with us. For the whole of my Christian upbringing and the whole of my family life, I had honoured the holy tradition of the Sunday roast within the confines of the nuclear family. Sabbath was an inward-looking time of retreat from the world. Now, Sabbath was becoming, for me, a time of extroversion, a radical embrace of everything that was different. I would often remind the folk that this was just how Jesus had lived out his life: eating and drinking with anyone who was hungry for the abundant life. And it was within the radical informality of these gatherings that much of his most profound teaching took place. This was a taste not just of good soup; this was a taste of 24/7 living, Jesus style, and foretaste of the Messianic Banquet that awaits us all at the end of time, and I was loving every minute of it.

Lottie & Michael

Chapter nineteen

Three Men Swimming

One day, when I was at Roy and Pashey's home, she shared with me an extraordinary experience that she had had a few weeks earlier. By now I had become familiar with the way in which Romanies share such experiences. First, they take great care to set the scene, ensuring that the listener is focused and able to picture for themselves what has happened. Only then is the narrative unfolded. Pashey explained, at some length, how she had come home from a birthday party and had a strong cup of coffee. She had then fallen asleep on her bed, only to wake up a little later. What she then saw was so fantastic that she immediately felt the need to check out that she was not hallucinating or simply losing her marbles. Once she had confirmed, in her own mind, that she was fully awake and of sound mind, she yielded to what to what she was experiencing...

On the ceiling above her, writing began to appear and roll past her eyes. The words were in several strange foreign scripts that she did not understand. This went on for some time. After a bit she asked God to give her some clue as to what the words meant. For some time nothing changed and there were only the strange foreign words in strange scripts.

Then, three words appeared in English:

"......three men swimming......"

This was followed, a little later, by another strange word:

"......stiger......"

I have to say that when Pashey first told me of this experience, a measure of western scepticism came over me. This kind of thing has its place in the book of Daniel, but who has ever heard of anything like this in our day? Pashey asked me if I had any idea what the meaning of this experience might be. I said I had no idea at all but that we should simply wait and see if, in the fullness of time, anything became clear.

As time went by, I almost forgot about Pashey's writing on the ceiling experience. Although I took all the experiences the Romanies reported to me very seriously, I felt it was important to try and discern carefully which of the phenomena were of God and which could be explained in some other way. Perhaps the writing Pashey had seen was in the latter category. But then, one evening some months later, young Charlotte had popped over the road to offer an explanation to the words "three men swimming".

We had recently had further baptisms of a Romany family and three young men who had joined us. The young men were in fact Afghan refugees who had clearly made a commitment to following Jesus. These baptisms had taken place at the back of Church House where Frank had placed a bath on the grass. These three young men were the three men swimming! And perhaps, the different scripts Pashey had seen, represented their different dialects.

Samie, Rahmon & Sohrab together with Abraham's family

I have come to see the arrival of these young men in our community as quite significant. They, rather like the Romanies, were exiles, people who were seeking acceptance in a strange and foreign culture. As asylum seekers they were deeply needy. They quickly became part of our Friday evening Romany Cluster and friendships developed across the not insignificant language barriers. This all led to further baptisms and confirmations. This time, Bishop Stephen was to confirm nine Romanies and three Afghans in Canterbury Cathedral on 4 November 2008.

Outside Canterbury Cathedral

The word that had appeared on the ceiling at the end of the revelation Pashey had seen was "stiger". For some time it remained an enigma, to the point that we almost forgot it. But then it occurred to me to inquire of the Afghan boys and, after some research, they told us that the word "stiger" probably meant "others". This seemed to make sense: "three men swimming … and others". These were surely the two other Afghan boys who had later joined us and who were then baptised on a later occasion.

Was Pashey's experience of the writing on the ceiling one way of God keeping us on our spiritual toes? The verification of any prophecy comes only retrospectively, when the first word is confirmed later by events that unfold on the ground. Scripture tells us, "where there is no vision, the people perish". [35] The Afghans and the Romanies are people

---

[35] Proverbs 29:18 KJB

who have lost hope of a future beyond their present.   This prophecy had the effect of raising our level of expectation, of waiting to see what God might do next.

Chapter twenty

A Harvest of Souls

Frank baptised into Christ

The baptism of Frank, Naomi and their five children, Charlene, Champ, Kelley-Rose, Naomi and Pro, was another highlight of the year 2008. The family, together with Rachel - a Romany girl from Ashford -and the parents of a child from a *gorgia* family, all asked for baptism on the very Sunday we had appointed for our Harvest service. This had traditionally been a joint service with both 9.30 and 11.15 congregations coming together for a 10.30 service. Much planning and careful thinking would be necessary beforehand.

Now that Cranbrook School swimming pool was shut for the winter we needed to find another way of baptising by full immersion. Frank produced a paddling pool that we inflated in the West End porch and then filled with water using two very long hosepipes that came right across the church from a tap in the East to the pool in the West. Though ingenious, this solution was almost as eccentric as the eighteenth-century full immersion font that I described earlier. But I was convinced that the pastoral need of the people to have full immersion baptism should take precedent over other concerns. However, as some members of the congregation might have a problem with baptisms in the West Porch, I decided that this part of the ceremony would be performed after the main service had come to an end.

In the event, we had another quite different problem to deal with. The whole nave roof was being re-leaded that autumn and a temporary plastic tent had been put in place over the scaffolding to keep the rain out of the church whilst the works were in progress. However, as we gathered for our Harvest service, driving rain was sweeping across the Weald and the plastic tent proved quite inadequate to keep the water out. As the service progressed many were getting wet in the pews.

Over forty Romanies came along to our Harvest service that day to support Frank and his family and this made it possible for me to lay hold of the opportunity to tell the story of the Romany awakening of faith that had been unfolding in our midst. Going right back to 1999, I brought to the front each person and their family, one by one, recalling every event from the vicarage holly, the light from the tower, the burning bush and the heavenly music, right through to the present moment.

I had a deep conviction that this story was simply too extraordinary and too precious to go untold. This is how the Apostles must have felt as they witnessed the signs and wonders God was performing in their day. "As for us", they said, "we cannot help speaking about what we have seen and heard!"[36]

Traditional Harvest services are usually given over to a celebration of God's creation and thanksgiving for a successful harvest. However, it was clear to me that the New Testament never sees creation as an

---

[36] Acts 4:20

71

end in itself. Rather, the themes of sowing and reaping are always understood by Jesus as metaphors for understanding the unseen, but very real spiritual world. Yes, we had food on our plates every day and should be thankful to God for that. But far more important in the eyes of the Apostles was the great harvest of souls that would be reaped following the proclamation of the Good News of Jesus Christ. More had been baptised that year at St Dunstan's than for many years, and this was something to marvel at and to rejoice in.

Since nearly all of these new converts came from the Romany community, there were very real parallels to be drawn with the story of the early church, where large numbers of gentiles were incorporated into the existing Jewish-Christian community. Much of the New Testament is given over to a consideration of the many issues that arise when we take seriously Jesus' command to go to all ethnic groups on earth and make disciples of them, baptising them in the name of the Father, the Son and the Holy Ghost[37]. The influx of Romanies into church that day brought many of these issues to the surface.

Whilst the 11.15 community was learning, week by week, how to adapt to the newcomers, this was the first time that those from the 9.30 congregation had experienced anything of the sort. Our Romanies are not versed in the niceties of Anglican ritual, order and propriety. They feel free to arrive when they like, wander in and out of church according to their needs, and chat. The most poignant moment came during Holy Communion when the priest invites the people to come forward and receive the sacrament. Our robed choir processed round, as is their custom, to receive before everyone else. However, on this occasion, all the Romanies came to the front all at once, like children hungry for food. The choir's passage back to their stalls was blocked and it was all very embarrassing for a few moments.

When everything is suddenly quite different from the normal run of things, a primordial fear sometimes surfaces and people feel overwhelmed and unable to cope. Can the God they have known and reverenced all their lives possibly wish things to happen like this? Looking back, I now see this as both pastoral failure on my part, and

---

[37] Matthew 28:19

what St Paul called "the birth pangs of the new creation."[38] I should have foreseen these problems and prepared each of the communities for each other. But of this I am equally certain: it would have been a mistake to quench the Spirit and keep everything nice and orderly at all costs. Some of these issues I explore more fully in a later chapter.

The decision to have the actual baptisms *after* the service proved right. I led the candidates, their godparents, families and friends, out of the nave and into the West Porch, playing "we are marching in the light of God" on sopranino recorder all the way with Ben Bentham strumming along on guitar. The porch was just big enough for those being baptised and their godparents and close relatives. I spoke of the "harvest of righteousness" that would be forthcoming in the lives of each candidate as the Holy Spirit would bring forth the fruit of the Spirit over the years to come. The deep waters of death were indeed icy cold that day, but as Frank and Naomi rose to new life, all our hearts were warmed in a quite unexpected way. For Frank's brother, Aaron, who had brought his guitar with him, began to lead us in song. Another service had begun; unplanned and quite spontaneous! This then overflowed into a soup lunch in Church House that Roy had decided to prepare when we were all in the service. The planned bring-and-share lunch for all in church had quite understandably been abandoned, no doubt due to the waters of chaos that continued to pour through our nave roof and flood areas of the church.

The occasion had been as surreal as it had been blessed and, at a church meeting after the event there was considerable tension in the air. The chief concerns voiced were quite legitimate in their own right, and centered around health and safety issues. Further matters were raised. Had allowance been made for the extra cost on water rates for such a large volume of water? Was I aware that one of the Romany children had sworn? What did the story of the Romanies have to do with Harvest? I went home deeply troubled in my spirit and wept. For not one had mentioned the wonder of so many coming to faith and being added to our number.

---

[38] Romans 8:22

"Many waters cannot quench love; rivers cannot wash it away".[39]

Naomi baptised into Christ

---

[39] Song of Songs 8:9

Chapter twenty one

The Bread of Life

By Autumn 2008, over forty Romanies had been baptised into Christ within a year. Sustaining them on the journey of faith became, for me, an ever-urgent question. Some years earlier at St Dunstan's we had spent a year and a half exploring the merits of allowing children to receive the Holy Communion prior to confirmation. In the end we came to a common mind: providing that both the children and their parents had had some instruction in the meaning of the sacrament, and that the parents thought their children to be ready, these children were welcome to receive the bread, having perhaps dipped it in the wine first.

The whole debate had centered around whether the grace of God only comes to a person if they have an intellectual understanding of the meaning of communion or whether the grace of God cannot be limited in that way. I was strongly persuaded by the latter view for, after all, we had for some years been giving the bread and the wine to Natalie, a severely disabled young person in the congregation and we regularly took the sacrament into our local care home where many of the adults were scarcely aware of what was going on when the bread was put in their mouths. The grace of God would always surpass our human understanding.

Never was the case stronger for offering the bread unconditionally than with the Romanies. They thought and acted not as individual thinking machines, but as extended families who shared the same commitment to Christ, and who had often all been baptised into His risen life on one and the same occasion. What could be more natural than to put the bread into the outstretched hand of little Derby Smith when he looked you in the eye with a smile? What could be more profoundly wrong than to send him away empty-handed and confused in his little mind as to why, at home, he would be offered bread but at church he would be denied it?

But, more importantly, we came to understand that, for the Romanies, faith was not a matter of responding with spoken words of assent to propositional statements of faith that we might put to them. Rather, faith was an all-embracing, holistic experience that gathered up everything in a person's life. The Cartesian body-mind dualism that has been the curse of our culture for four hundred years is something the Romanies know nothing of. Eating and drinking together is what Jesus did with his friends as naturally as they did. When I celebrate communion, I simply set the scene of the last supper for them in the most simple terms possible. The full force of Jesus' dramatic statement that the bread is his body and the wine his blood is a spiritual reality that the Romanies then seem to embrace without difficulty. I began to ask myself whether they understood what is going on in communion at a deeper level than I, in spite of all my years of theological education and pondering of the holy mysteries. In the same way that the waters of baptism had powerfully brought home for them the drama of death and rebirth, so the bread and the wine were potent signs that are as real as the very things they signify. It is not so much that they point beyond themselves to another purely spiritual reality; such a way of thinking would be alien to the Romany world-view. Rather, they are - for the community that receive with a lively faith - the very body and blood of Jesus. It would be pointless for me to attempt to explain to them, for example, the arguments over the meaning of Holy Communion, which fuelled the Reformation. It is a problem that they don't have and don't need to be given.

Earlier in the year of 2008, I had become aware of something similar on two other occasions. The first was Ash Wednesday.

Many folk could not make it to the actual service on the day, so I decided to repeat the ceremony of ashing on the following Sunday of Lent 1. The way the Romanies entered into this made a deep impression on me. They each received, with great seriousness, the sign of the cross I made on their foreheads with the ash. I had explained how we all came from dust and ashes, and that we would return to the same. Ash meant death. Sin was spiritual death. So sin was ash. Jesus had put things right by going through death on the cross for all of us. To carry the mark of ash on our foreheads was to remember all of this. What then bowled me over was the way the older children insisted that I mark the foreheads of the tiny ones present, some of whom were strapped into buggies. This was not a joke for the older children. Everyone had to be included, from the youngest to the oldest. If the ash was true for one, it was true for all.

A little later in Lent that year, I put together a labyrinth in the chancel using chairs, ropes, and a whole variety of symbols and pictures. Each of the twenty-four stations represented a different point in John's Gospel, starting with the raising of Lazarus and continuing on to the empty tomb. There was everything from a doll's house representing the rooms in the house that Jesus would prepare for each one of us, to the vinegar given to Jesus on the cross. I realized that I had, unwittingly, struck upon a way of communicating the whole passion narrative using as few words as possible and as many symbols as I could find. For Rachel and her family this struck a chord and several *gorgia* members of the congregation delighted in explaining each station in the half-hour long labyrinth journey to the Romany children. Later, Rachel shared with me her sense of the Holy Spirit filling her whole body at certain points along the way and I encouraged her to reflect on what God was saying to her at these particular stations.

Chapter twenty two

The Shadow Side

"[Jesus] ministered in weakness, under a shadow as it were.
This is, however, how authentic mission always presents itself – in weakness." [40]

So far, this narrative has focused on the extraordinary blessings that God has poured out on the Romanies in these times. However, as I got to know them and their stories better, I became ever more aware of the very dark shadow side of their existence. The song that follows was written some time ago by Derby Smith, after whom Roy and Pashey had named their fifth born son.[41] Moses felt that it was very important for me to hear a CD of this song, for the words tell the story of how things had been for the previous generation of Romany travellers, prior to their settlement in more permanent accommodation.

Pastor Lywood would have been only too familiar with the kind of collective depression that hung over the people he ministered to. To be a nomadic people was at once a joy and a curse. To be forever on the move was both a conscious choice and a necessity, as successive councils moved the Romanies on from site to site. There were many consequences of the nomadic life. Children growing up would constantly have their education interrupted with the result that they remained illiterate and so unable to enter the mainstream of society. But, above all, there was the unrelenting hounding, marginalizing, vilifying and scape-goating of them by the *gorgios,* who would not allow them to find a place within the broader community. The song has a jolly lilt to it but the words betray a spirit of despair and, at the end, even a death wish. Would life in heaven free them from the oppression they knew on earth?

---

[40] David Bosch, *Transforming Mission* page 49
[41] The name Derby is derived from the famous annual *Epsom Derby.*

"Tonight as I stay by the roadside,
Just watching those travellers go by,
Thinking, what will become of those travellers
Whenever their time comes to die.

There's a Master up yonder in Heaven
Got a place that we might call our home
But will we have to work for a living?
Or shall we continue to roam.

Will there be any travellers in Heaven?
Any places at which we might stay?
Will there be any gavvers[42] or Councils
To move our old trailers away?

Will the gorgios[43] join with those travellers?
Will we always have money to spare?
Will they have respect for those Gypsies
In a land that lies hidden up there?

Will there be any travellers in Heaven?
Any pubs where we might get some beer?
Will there be the same old landlords
Who say, 'Sorry. No Gypsies served here.'

Will the travellers have to keep roaming?
Will we have to keep roaming around?
I'm so tired of roaming this country
I'd rather be under the ground." [44]

Whilst some of the details of this song represent what, at least in England, is largely a bygone age, the legacy of those dark days lives on in the settled communities across the South East. Meanwhile, the plight of the Romanies in Eastern Europe and Russia has worsened since the

---

[42] *gavvers* (or *gaffers*) = bosses
[43] *gorgios* = non-Gypsies.
[44] Derby Smith, Epsom, Surrey

fall of communism and the rise, in some places of neo-fascism. The international "credit crunch" is being offered as an explanation for the new wave of persecution of minority ethnic groups that is now being reported. Whilst anti-Semitism may not be as widespread as in earlier generations, amongst those now most vulnerable to persecution are the Romanies. I have heard their treatment in England described as "the last socially acceptable form of racism". Though the current situation here is clearly much better than in many other countries, much still needs to be done before they are fully accepted in our communities. I share the following experience, which is not uncommon.

One afternoon, the winter sun was out and I offered to take Charlotte, Charlene and two of the Afghan boys down to the seaside at Hastings. We had a lovely time sitting on the beach near the pier, watching the waves and enjoying each other's company. To finish the trip off, I invited them all to a cup of tea on the veranda of a hotel facing the sea. After about half an hour, the respectable couple, who had been sitting at the table next to us got up to leave. I asked the gentleman if he would be willing to take a photo of our group. He turned to me and pointed at the two Romany girls. "Are you sure you want to have the glass on your camera cracked?" he said. I was so shocked I felt I must surely have misheard what he said. I asked him to repeat what he had said. He simply took the picture you see on the next page and left.

The girls confirmed that I had correctly heard what he said. To my amazement, they seemed quite unfazed and commented calmly, "it's racism, isn't it Martin." A few minutes later I felt a wave of feeling arise within me and began to weep. The others gathered around me and put me back together. Later, in the car on the way home, Charlotte had had a chance to reflect on how this incident had affected me. "It's very rare, Martin, that anyone notices what people say about us," she said.

My tears were not an indulgence or a sign of moral weakness. They were a sign of moral outrage. Back at Charlotte's home we reflected together further on those racist words and one of the Afghan boys commented, with some degree of passion, "we have to love these people. It is the only way!" The boys knew from their own experience of persecution, just how the girls were feeling. We determined that we would not be overcome by evil, rather we would overcome evil with good.[45]

---

[45] Romans 12:21

Martin, Charlene, Charlotte, Raman & Sohrab in Hastings

As the local vicar in our little market town I found myself well placed to make a difference to how the Romanies were regarded and able to make links with a variety of organizations on their behalf. One Romany man, whose family I had got to know well, pleaded with me to go to court with him in Sittingbourne on a couple of Wednesdays. I wondered whether this was a legitimate use of my time when, after all, I was supposed to be on duty every Wednesday morning at the communion service. I asked myself, 'What kind of God is it we serve? If he is a God willing to leave the ninety-nine to go the rescue of the one, then I shouldn't I be free to do the same?'

On the long journey to court I became aware that my friend really needed me alongside him in his hour of trial. As he explained at great length the case against him, it seemed to me that he had been singled out as an offender in a quite unfair, petty and prejudiced way. At court, I was able to play a role in helping communication between the solicitor and my friend and, on the second occasion, I was invited by the judge to offer evidence in support of my friend's situation. This seemed to make a real difference and we went home praising God for the positive outcome. My presence as a clergyman supporting one of society's more vulnerable people seemed to count in the eyes of the court.

Several of the local Romanies have asked me if I could help them with issues regarding their accommodation. In some cases, it was simply a matter of writing to the housing authorities to plead for a larger house in view of the number of children in the family. In a number of other cases, it was to defend local Romanies against allegations that had been made against them in the neighbourhood. For example, one young, single Romany woman had been accused of providing accommodation for three other Romany relatives. She was told that her benefit would stop if this continued. To my certain knowledge there is not a shred of evidence to support these fabrications. We never discovered who had trumped up such lies and what their inner motives might be. Speaking to those responsible for the housing of minority ethnic groups helped me to become more aware of the long-standing issues surrounding the housing of the Romanies in these parts.

Allegations of petty theft also came my way and I did my best to help local police and others come to a sensible way of handling what may have happened. Part of the problem here is that the Romanies have a much more highly developed sense of shared-ownership than *gorgios* do. What for us is theft, may sometimes be seen by them as borrowing. Some of the children were not fully aware of the different ways the two communities understand these things. A mobile phone, for example, may be widely shared within extended Romany families. When I phone a number I am often not sure whom I will find myself speaking to. However, within my culture, personal possessions are clung onto much more tenaciously. A crucial part of the education of Romany children is about helping them to understand these differences and to know where the boundaries lie within each of the two cultures.

My longstanding links with the head teachers of our local schools were also very useful. Pooling insights into the young people in our care made it possible to share oversight of the fragile lives of some of the Romany children. Much hinges on how seriously the parents take the need for their children to develop the literacy skills that had been denied them when they themselves were young. One of the most common charges I hear against the Romanies is that they are parasitic on society, failing to take jobs and earn a proper income of their own and living at the expense of hard-working tax-payers. But the Romanies of the older generation are in a Catch Twenty-Two situation. However dearly they might wish to find regular employment, they are denied the possibility because they lack the necessary literacy skills and are not trusted by the community at large. Some of the younger women have told me how they cannot find employment, even at the local supermarket. This all raises the imperative of sustained education for the children, in the hope that they will ultimately be able to find - and retain - regular jobs.

I felt increasingly that it would be very important, in the long term, for the Romany community to secure their own representation on some of the local bodies. I had been invited to join the new Cranbrook Community Group, which was made up of people working in every sector of the life of the town and I asked the chairperson if I could bring Pashey along with me to represent the Romanies. This was warmly welcomed and, on arrival, it became clear that Pashey was already well known to lots of folk in the room. This was the ideal forum in which key community issues could be looked at and mutual respect between the community at large and the Romanies deepened. Certainly, some present were seeing the Christian commitment that many Romanies were making, as a sign of their determination to be more fully part of the whole community. Again, I was pleased that, as parish priest, I had been able to bring together things that might otherwise have remained dangerously separate.

However, the sense of hopelessness that some Romanies feel and the conviction that their situation will never improve, causes them to live in the moment and not make plans for the future. This is the shadow side of their wonderful freedom from the tyranny of a life controlled by a *chronos* understanding of time.

For instance, it was only after getting to know one family very well that I finally plucked up the courage to confront them over their smoking. I felt that smoking was, at least in one sense, a failure to think of the future consequences of the habit. It was a kind of collapsing of time into the present sensory pleasure of the moment. They all knew only too well the health hazards of smoking but would argue that, when a person's time is up, then he will die anyway.

At first I talked only with one of the daughters in the family. She felt the challenge and over a short period of time was able to cut right back with the help of much prayer and plenty of nicotine chewing gum. The desire to quit then moved on to her mother. At first, dad was very reluctant to consider giving up, having been a chain smoker since his childhood. However, after a few months the whole family home became smoke free for a time and I enjoyed my visits to them even more. I had thought long and hard about how to break open this subject with them. The argument that their bodies were not their own but collectively formed a temple for the Holy Spirit, proved to be the right kind of incarnational approach. The Holy Spirit did not want to get a cough in a smoky temple, did He!

This chapter has drawn attention to the darker, shadow side of Romany life as it is today. Whilst the situation of which Derby Smith sang is largely a thing of the past, the collective subconscious of the Romanies keeps something of this spirit alive even now that times have improved. I want to finish with a testimony from Roy Smith of an extremely dark spiritual experience he had in 1990 as a young man. I recorded his words and then transcribed the exact text. The use of repetition and the sheer simplicity of the language in its roughest form help to convey the way a Romany passes on to others their deepest experiences of the heart.[46]

---

[46] Rolland Allen comments of value of testimony:
"Upon the speaker, too, the effort to express his truth exercises a profound effect. The expression of his experience intensifies it; it renews it; it repeats it; it enlightens it. In speaking of it he goes through it again; in setting it before another he sets it before himself in a new light. He gets a deeper sense of its reality and power and meaning. In speaking of it he pledges himself to the conduct and life which it involves. He proclaims himself bound by it, and every time that his speech produces an effect upon another, that effect reacts upon himself, making his hold upon his truth surer and stronger." p.11
Rolland Allen *"The Spontaneous Expansion of the Church and the causes which hinder it". Chapter 2 "The Nature and Character of Spontaneous Expression."* 1927

Roy

"I would like to share with others a very remarkable experience that I once had.

One day I went to lay down on my mother's bed to have a rest. While I were dead, something very remarkable happened to me. For some unknown reason I found myself in a very, very strange, weird, very, very frightened dark place. I'm not too sure at the time I were dreaming, and I'm not too very sure I weren't dreaming, cos is were such a sort of short time after I went to lay down. I had felt myself in a very dark place ... on my own ... and I was really, really, frightened.

Then I noticed, that I was in 'ell the devil, Satan. The place that I were I had noticed either side of me in this lonely, lonely dark footpath that I was beginning to walk, that in the past there were people that had already been there and died when they'd been there for so long, punished. While I was walking along this dark, lonely path, I had also noticed on my left and right there were people there at the time being chained, were chained, and they were begging to me for 'elp. Very, very, very 'elp they was asking, asking and begging for mercy like nothing like it. I had never 'eard anything like it in my life.

Then I noticed again while I were walking people were screaming, crying, begging, just for mercy to get of the place they were. Then I had noticed that I was in 'ell with the devil.

Along the way that I did walk and started to run from this lonely foot path, feeling that I didn't want to be there myself, I had noticed little gold arrows, coming past my 'ead from the back of me. Then when I looked I had noticed it was Satan trying to shoot me with these arrows. Then I started to run in panic, really did start to run in panic, and I started to run and run and run as much as I could run, and the devil was running behind me following me as fast as I could run. Then after a long, long, long way of running it seemed to me that the path never got any shorter or there was no ending to it. It just seemed to get longer really. But I still kept running as much as I could with all my strength; I was feeling really, really exhausted ... really windless and weak ... then after running for such a long time ... maybe... I can't actually say how far I did run... I noticed from out of the blues, I noticed a little small light.

Then I thought to myself I got to make it to this light ... as much as I can ... if I can, while the devil was still on my back shooting these arrows at me trying very hard to hit me with these arrows. I really think he wanted to caught me so I could stay where I were. So I kept running and running and running then I finally after a long time being so exhausted and so weak come to the light and when I come to the light I looked through the light and I looked up and there was a massive, massive mountain of broken rocks that I had to climb through the light to get to the top. Then I started to climb up through this mountain up these rocks into the light, noticed that the devil had come out of the dark with me into the light up on this rock ,so I finally climbed and climbed and climbed with a lot of struggle, struggle and effort, if I were so weak and exhausted I finally made it to the top of this rock, these brocken rocks to the top.

Then what happened I come to a place that there were no trees no flowers no houses no animals there wasn't anything that I would have noticed it were just like a plain, flat … desert, really but though it were such a pretty place and so peaceful … nothing that I've experienced before like it to be honest.

Then what I did I started to run as fast as I could, even though I was still in the light I was still too feared and too frightened of the devil and from where I come from, so I started to run and run and run, and I had noticed that the devil was still on the back of me running and still shooting his arrows and how his arrows had not of hit me I don't know they were just coming past me one side from the other. Then after running for such a little, while I had noticed there were someone on a cart being pulled with a donkey at the time, there was a donkey pulling with someone on a cart from a distance from where I were. So what I did I started to run towards it as fast as I could … so I got so close after running, and the devil were still on my back trying to shoot me with these arrows. Then I become to the cart and noticed there were a man on the cart 'olding these reigns of the donkey whilst the donkey was pulling him and at the back of the cart there was some small rocks that he had loaded himself or someone 'ad loaded from him really.

Then I has says to 'im "Sir! Please could you 'elp me? Look!" I said "the devil is trying to shoot me with these arrows: he's trying to kill me. Please Sir, could you 'elp me?" Then what the man did on the cart, he did not spoke to me out his mouth. He had spoken to me through my mind, and said "No! No one can 'urt you when you are with me. No!" And what he did, he looked at me and shook 'is 'ead and the moment the man shook 'is 'ead everything that 'appened to me, from coming out of 'ell from the dark, and from being chased for such a long time and so exhausted and so worried and so distressed, and so feared that the devil was going to get me … the moment the man shook 'is 'ead, everything that I knew was forgotten and it did no longer existed.

Now, he was a plain looking man with a brown beard a shawl over his 'ead and pretty blue eyes. From that day until this day I believe in my 'eart, that it was the Christ, because who could just shake is 'ead and make be forget about such a terror and such exhausted and such being a-frightened that I were. All the man did was shook 'is 'ead at me and told me in my mind: "No!" He said. "No one can 'urt you when you are with me!"

Then what I did I had put my 'and up on the cart and I 'ad lifted myself on the cart beside him sitting and I rode with 'im beside 'im down through the dessert and as being round about 17 to 18 years ago, I am sure, and I have never forgot that experience and personally in meself, I don't think I would ever forget it. Because there was a time I was in so much danger and in so much darkness and in so much fear … and just looking at a man at another moment at another time and going through all of that, just by 'im shaking 'is 'ead at me and making me forget everything didn't exist, to me was something that no one else could ever do but the Christ, and I believe within my heart, that it was the Christ that I were talking to and I believe in my heart, that I rid on the cart with Jesus.

Now if there's anything that I have spoken about that's not true or if there is anything that I have said that maybe … it was just a dream … then I can only say to God in Jesus name "forgive me", but I know what I experienced, I know what I saw and where I ended up at the end. No one can look at you and say "No! No one can hurt you when you are with me" … who else do anyone know if it weren't for Jesus, and in my mind and in my heart I will always say it were Jesus on the cart and it were Jesus who saved me from Satan. Thank you Jesus! Amen."

Chapter Twenty Three

Tribe and Tribalism

By the autumn of 2008, it was clear that we were in contact with an ever-growing number of Romanies. First Pashey, and later Charlotte, carefully helped me draw up a huge family tree including most of their relatives and covering four generations. Aaron, whom they were still mourning, had been father to nine children, and grandfather to at least around forty grandchildren. And this was only one part of the broader dynasty! The internal relationships were especially deep since several sisters from one family had married the brothers of another family. Every person in the dynasty clearly knew every single name represented on the family tree and the circumstances of that person.

Several things make it hard for the outsider to understand Romany relationships. A man could, for example, choose to take his mother's surname for his family name if he wished. Many children were named after their father, mother, or another relative, and the pool of names they drew on was quite small. On one occasion, I remember there being at least three Abrahams in church and, at one Friday cluster, we had no fewer that four Moses present! On another, three Reuben's and four Charlotte's! To identify an individual, a prefix or suffix is often added to make clear which person is meant. For example, Rachel refers to "my sister Mary" to distinguish her from "my daughter Mary". To distinguish sons from their fathers, I began to refer to "big Roy" or "little Roy", "big Moses" or "little Moses". Lottie's son is "Marky-boy." However, Charlotte, Lottie and Charlene seem almost interchangeable as names. The very small pool of names serves to further heighten the sense of tribal identity and clan, though I have yet to discover why the men, in particular, are so often given Old Testament names. One theory, as exotic as it is unverifiable, is that the Romanies are one of the lost tribes of Israel.

Communication through the network of relations is constant and happens almost exclusively through word of mouth. Impromptu visits across the South East take place all the time as personal news is shared at a deep level and passed on. These families are, therefore, deeply dependant on their cars and vans, which they keep up and running on extremely limited resources. I have yet to find a Romany home with a telephone landline. Mobiles are becoming more common but they are often out of credit. Calls made are always very short to keep the cost down. All this helps to preserve a face-to-face mode of communication that is closer to that of the Middle-ages, than of the twenty-first century. Whilst the rest of us struggle to hold at bay the waves of emails, voice-mail messages and correspondence, the Romanies remain in a blessed time warp, a place where communication from the heart is the only known way. Cut off from the information-overload of society at large, they remain unaware of events happening both on their doorstep and afar. This all throws them back on each other.

Trip to the Northiam Oasts

Through such an intimate network of relationships the grace of God is free to flow in remarkable ways. One event in particular served to illustrate this for me. At the generous behest of Sir Christopher and Georgie Wates, I organized a coach trip to take us to the Christian retreat centre at the Northiam Oasts. From the moment we headed off, there was an extraordinary sense of celebration, of sheer delight at being on the move. Arriving at the Oasts was like arriving in heaven – but with none of the "gavvers or councils" to spoil the fun as Derby Smith had feared in his song! The kids went for a swim in the indoor pool and then we all enjoyed a wonderful meal before it came to the speeches. I shared the story of Pastor Lywood and said how I was sure he would be doing cartwheels in heaven as he looked down to see the seeds of faith that he had planted, all those years ago, coming to fruition in our day. Then, quite unexpectedly, little Roy Smith, aged ten, stood to make an impromptu speech, followed by his mother, Pashey, who spontaneously began to sing a song she had just conceived in her heart.

For all their tribal spirit and inwardness, I was struck by how these Romanies were able to "adopt" the several *gorgios* who had joined the trip. Notice for example, Charlie-Emma at the front of the picture above. There were also my wife and I, Paul and Chrissie (soon to be married), and Revd. Ben Bentham. This was surely a move of the Spirit, helping us to lay hold of the New Testament vision of a church in which differences of culture and ethnicity become incidental as, together, we discover our identity afresh in Christ.

> "There is neither Jew nor Gentle,
> neither slave nor free,
> neither male nor female,
> for you are all one in Christ Jesus."[47]

---

[47] Galatians 3:28

Pashey & Chris Wates

Pashey & Ben Bentham

Integrating the two cultures is, however, always a challenge, as became clear when it came to the celebration of my 57th birthday. I had mentioned in passing that this was coming up and, without any hesitation, the Romanies offered to organize the entire event for me! We booked the sixth form centre at Cranbrook School and I invited everyone I had contact with to come along if they would like to. Mark, Lottie's partner, set up the sound equipment and we had country and western music as well as live music from Pashey, Absolom, Leo and Diego. Lots of sandwiches had been prepared and brought in and we waited to see who would roll up.

Martin's 57th

Romanies from across Kent arrived, many of whom I only knew as names on my family tree. They came straight into the centre of things and were fully at home. Meanwhile, two other groups arrived from St Dunstan's. Those who attend the formal services settled down at one end of the long room and those who attend the informal service remained at the other end. There were therefore *three* quite distinct groups. A few of us moved from group to group but it didn't prove possible to achieve that same sense of unity that we had enjoyed on the Northiam trip. Clearly, fear of the outsider goes very deep in the human psyche, especially if that outsider dresses, speaks and acts quite differently.

At our October Harvest Barn Dance in the Vestry Hall, however, we made some progress, for although there were once again the same three distinct groupings of people in the Vestry Hall that night, and although each group continued to gravitate back into its own comfort zones, the discipline and givenness of the barn dance drew everyone present together in a remarkable way. This was how I reflected on the event in the parish magazine:

> "This year's Harvest Barn Dance was a real triumph and sent me home with much food for thought. It was wonderful to see folk from every part of our community coming together to celebrate. Although three distinct social groups huddled together in different parts of the Vestry Hall, once the dance got going most took to the floor and we transcended ourselves.
>
> All dance is liberating, even if you're like me and you don't know your left foot from your right. However, there is something about barn dance, which is quite unique. I am sure it must have emerged as a means of helping a community to flatten out differences of class, social pecking order and blood ties. It even has something inherently healing about it. Feuding parties over the generations must surely have seen, even if only for a moment, the silliness of their ways. For in barn dance everyone is suddenly equal, everyone has to relate to everyone else, and a synergy is generated in which the total becomes greater than the sum of the parts.
>
> As soon as the dance comes to an end, folk retreat into their safe huddles once again. But the memory of the dance lingers on. Those who took to the floor had the courage to step out of their comfort zones and to actually hold hands with the other, twist and turn, look each other in the eye, laugh over each other's mistakes and delight in the ones who come to the

rescue. Together, we catch a glimpse of how community can feel and perhaps go on our way home wondering why on earth it is not like that at other times.

But, we are on earth and not in heaven and life is not always a ball. In heaven, the eternal dance of the Trinity continues unceasingly as Father, Son and Holy Spirit weave in and out of each other in perfect harmony. The life of heaven overshadows us at those moments when we set aside our cultural straightjackets and allow the freedom of the Godhead to break in. The formality and the givenness of the barn dance help hugely in providing a safe framework in which we can experiment with a more excellent way of living, just for a moment. Taking the risk to let go provides God with an opportunity he must surely relish. I picture Father, Son and Holy Spirit joining the dance and gently helping the process forward. Barn dance is in fact *liturgy*, or "the work of the people," to go to the root meaning of the word.

I am fearful that, in trying to explain what is going on, I may be taking away some of the magic. The best lovemaking (for that is what it is) needs no words. But my prayer is that something of what we laid hold of during that Harvest Celebration might stay with us and inform our day-to-day life. I know that the best wine comes only at the end of the party. But it would be a pity if we had to wait till heaven till we understood what Jesus meant by "life in all its fullness".

Chapter Twenty-four

Romany Leaders' Retreat - Northiam Oasts

Rachel, Roy, Pashey, Moses, Reuben, Derby

At the Northiam Oasts

Just before Christmas 2008, I took two Romany families away with me on retreat to the Northiam Oasts. They had fond memories of the place from the coach outing we had had there just two months earlier but had yet to experience the full glories of a real retreat. Once again, we were so indebted to Sir Christopher Wates and his wife Georgie, who had made this possible. By now they were well known to the Romanies and Georgie had begun to take some of them under her wing as godmother.

The purpose of the retreat was firstly to spend quality time away from it all with one another, and secondly to intensify the leadership training that I had begun with Moses and Pashey earlier in the Autumn. In the next chapter we will explore the whole leadership dimension. But first

I will unfold some of the testimonies that surfaced in our group in the quietness of the evenings once most of the kids had just about gone to bed.

Pashey shared something that she had kept quietly on her heart until the retreat. She took us back to Lent 2007, the same period I referred to earlier when we had had the ashing ceremony and the labyrinth. During that Lent we had also run a Week of Accompanied Prayer at St Dunstan's and, every day, two prayer guides had gone up the road to work with the Romanies, helping them develop their prayer life. They had never before experienced anything quite like this and, not surprisingly, they opened their hearts to the discipline of meeting everyday with highly experienced guides.[48]

As Pashey looked back to her first day of that Week of Accompanied Prayer, she recalled how she had explained to her guide the difficulties she had with her spiritual life. Whilst on Sundays she would be really serious about Jesus, once Monday rolled round she recognized that her attitude towards Him had changed and that she was no longer attuned to his Spirit and focused on life in Him as she had been when in church. The guide encouraged Pashey to reflect on the moment in the Gospel when Jesus calls down the tax collector, Zacchaeus, from the sycamore tree and says to him:

"Today I must stay at your house!"[49]

Just as Zacchaeus's deepest desire had been to see Jesus with his own eyes, so Pashey longed to experience more of him in her daily life. Her guide suggested to Pashey that she might consider inviting Jesus to come and share her whole life with him, including absolutely everything: family, home, work, church meetings ... everything. She then went on to teach Pashey a new way of praying which involved breathing in the Holy Spirit and breathing out anything that is not of God. As she started to explore this new way of praying, she became aware of an extremely powerful white light on the right hand side of

---

[48] One of the guides was my dear friend, Richard King, who had focused his ministry for many years on spiritual direction. Richard was quite taken with the extraordinary openness of the Romanies to the spiritual dimension of life.
[49] Luke 19:5

her, though she felt it would have been inappropriate to turn her gaze towards the light.

The next day, when her guide returned, Pashey had a further remarkable experience as the session was unfolding. She became aware, once again, of the presence of a powerful light, but this time she felt that the light was emanating from a person who walked into the room and came and sat down next to her. She felt convinced this person was Jesus. Again she kept her eyes downwards but believed she saw one of his feet in a sandal as he walked past her; later she was able to describe exactly how the sandal looked. Pashey felt that she had invited Jesus into her home and that he had responded by making his presence felt in this extraordinary way. Again, she treasured up the whole experience in her heart.

Looking back on that revelation a year and a half later, Pashey came to believe that Jesus was seeking to reveal to her that His presence would, henceforth, be not just reserved to Sundays but would overflow into the whole of her life. The experience of Him as risen Lord - a powerful risen and abiding presence- was His way of responding to her heart's desire for more of Him. She felt the experience too precious, at the time, even to share with her prayer guide and too precious to share with anyone else until we were together, a year later, on our Northiam retreat. I suggested that this was a very wise decision, for she had needed a good long time to experience first-hand how the appearance of Jesus would actually change the day-to-day reality of her life. It was as though the authenticity of the experience would only be validated by any abiding change it might make in her life. To help us understand the biblical precedent for experiences of this kind, we read together the story of Jesus' Transfiguration on the mountain, when his clothes had shone a brilliant white - whiter than anyone could have bleached them[50]- and the revelation of the risen Jesus that John experienced whilst in exile on the island of Patmos[51].

Moses also shared with us that same evening at Northiam a profound experience that he had had many years earlier. The reader will remember

---

[50] Mark 9:2-13
[51] Revelation 1:12-20

Moses' 1998 experience of the light pouring into his living room from the church tower, the story with which this book began. Now, on retreat, Moses began to open out to us how things had once been for him.

For many years he had felt profoundly oppressed by malign spiritual forces that hounded him, night after night in nightmare form, causing him to groan in his sleep in a way that was distressing for his family. The height of this experience of evil came one night in early 1998 when he was driving home on his own and passing through Sissinghurst. From some distance he saw a nine-foot tall figure dressed in black, holding a fork in his hand and looking out over the road. Moses recalled how his hair literally stood on end at the sight. He was convinced this was Satan. He felt he had a choice at the time: he could keep going or yield to the evil. He made it home safely. Complete healing of his sense of being hounded by evil came finally and emphatically later that same year, on the night when the light shone from the church tower into his living room, into his life.

Recalling these hitherto deeply personal experiences and sharing them openly in the group when on retreat at Northiam had the effect of strengthening the faith of the whole group and preparing those of them who were being called into leadership.

Looking back over the retreat, one thing struck me very forcibly. Right up to the very last minute the whole thing was only ever a hair's breadth away from having to be cancelled. My dear friends had profound and deepening anxieties about leaving their homes and venturing forth into the unknown.

"What are we going to do all day long?"

"It's going to be so boring."

"We won't be able to sleep at night."

"We can't go because there will be no one to look after our dogs and ferrets."

"How will the children get to and fro from school?"

"We won't like the food."

"Who is paying for this?"

"Why do they want to pay for this?"

"Is this so you can write your book about us, Martin?"

All these murmurings reminded me of how it must have been for Moses of old as he was leading the Israelites through the wilderness and trying to excite them about a Promised Land they had never seen!

We spent many hours over several weeks working through all the issues that kept on resurfacing even after I had felt they had been carefully resolved. At the deepest level, I came to the conclusion that this people's experience of change had almost always been for the worse. Newness and the unknown are, for them, terrifying concepts; being out of control of their circumstances throws them into a panic. Even on the morning of our departure there were deep anxieties that their homes were not being left clean and tidy enough. The younger women were busy planning trips into town, fearful they would not cope with being away. It was only because we had built up a deep level of trust with each other, over a long period of time, that the trip was able to happen at all.

On arrival at the Oasts one of their chief concerns was about security at night. Who had the key to lock up the house? But, very slowly, they began to melt into the experience. They found the wonderful upper room and the prospect of time together there reminiscent of the TV show "Big Brother"! The quality of accommodation and food was of an order they had never imagined they would experience in their lives, and we talked a lot about how *some* wealthy people really do want to bless others. Many of their false assumptions about *gorgios* were thus challenged and turned around. When the Wates's came and shared with us one evening, we all realized that the one single unifying thing that brought us all together and that had ultimately made all things possible, was our shared love of Jesus. When the time came to go home, the person who had had the very gravest fears about the whole trip had visibly changed. "I would like to stay here for a whole month at least!"

> "There is no fear in love.
> But perfect love drives out fear,
> because fear has to do with punishment.
> The one who fears is not made perfect in love." [52]

---

9   1 John 4:18

Chapter twenty-five

Leadership Training

"…noninstitutionalised, nonstructured and nonorganised,
this response of theirs, as strange as it might seem to us,
must be recognized as the church,
or we are doing violence to Christianity.
Tillich says that beyond everything else,
the church is simply and primarily a group of people
who express a new reality by which they have been grasped". [53]

Training or cultural imperialism?

The retreat at Northiam had been planned, principally, to provide an opportunity for me to spend time training future Romany leaders. The single guiding principle that I had adopted for this work was this: the leadership had to be indigenous and thoroughly earthed within their culture. Any suggestion of imposing any other way on the Romanies would be cultural imperialism and an act of violence against the Gospel itself.

The first generation of the Christian church had had to address this issue head on. Once it had been established that the new gentile converts were full members of the Body of Christ alongside the Jewish believers, the church had to decide what place the Law of Moses would have in their lives. Famously, the Jerusalem Council (Acts 15) had ruled that gentile converts could not possibly be expected to undergo circumcision and have placed on their necks the full weight of the Mosaic Law. Such a move would not only kill dead the fledgling church, it would have been a denial of the incarnation itself. For, in taking human flesh, God had entered human history within a particular culture in order to bring the Good News to bear on a particular people. If Jesus had been born in Manhattan, he would have taken on that culture in order to transform it from within. At our camping weekend someone had said, "Jesus was

---

[53] Vincent Donovan p.84

a Romany!" This was another way of saying "we recognize in Jesus one of us. If he had been born in our day, and within our tribe, he would have looked like us, dressed like us, spoken like us, thought like us, and prayed like us."

And so, from the outset, I was aware of the very grave risk I was running in working with the Romanies. However conscious I may have been of the dangers of imposing my ways on them, I recognized that I would, unintentionally but inevitably, lead them in ways that would be alien to their culture. And so, from the beginning of my work with them, I had committed myself to instantly dropping anything I might say or do that was clearly not bearing any fruit.

Vincent Donovan had discovered, slowly and painfully over many years, that the Masai tribes' way of doing church would always be "noninstitutionalised, nonstructured and nonorganised". I made the same discovery with the Romanies. It was not that they rebelled when I found myself trying to organize them in any kind of formal way; it was simply that, for them, it was an alien way of thinking, being and doing. It was, you might say, ontologically impossible for them to "do formal". I had planned nicely, for example, that we were going to depart at 9.30am from Cranbrook to go to our Northiam retreat and that the first session would begin at 10.30am. The first session in fact began at noon and, in the event, I dropped what I had planned to do, simply because they were in a different place to where I might have liked them to be.

In truth, working in this way – or should I say playing in this way - had become a blessed relief and a wonderful novelty for me. I had become deeply disillusioned with the shadow side of rationalism and was searching out a new way of encountering God and learning about Him. And so, at a very deep level, the Romanies were my teachers, unwittingly running their own customized teaching programme just for me. This book has been typed-up by me. But it is really a Romany Epistle that they have written to me, an Epistle that reaches places in my heart that formal, institutional religion would never have been able to reach.

From time to time I pointed this out to them. When, for example, we were looking at the parable of the lost coin and the woman who swept her house clean in order to find it,[54] I shared that they were the ones with the brooms who, for some time, had been sweeping the dust and cobwebs out of my busy, cluttered and superficial life. The end result was that I found myself looking at a shiny coin in my hand, a coin that I had almost lost hope of ever finding. I think they found this affirming. Roy said "It is very sweet, Martin". As I entered the wide, open space of this new world, I remembered Jesus words:

> "As for what is inside you,
> be generous to the poor,
> and everything will be clean for you."[55]

Vincent Donovan writes of the grave error the institutional church had made in insisting that missionaries introduce the inherited Western pattern of doing church on the Masai tribes of Tanzania:

> "Missionaries are being told in effect, that they are not passing on the correct version of Christianity to these people if they do not build them their churches, write them a catechism, set up diocesan and chancery structures among them, establish seminaries, insure their financial future, and teach them the philosophy of the scholastics and the moderns, the morality of the Western churches, and the theology of Aquinas and Rahner. In effect another hundred year plan". [56]

Can God be taught?

My attempts at writing even a three-day plan - to use in our retreat at Northiam - proved unhelpful for me in my work with the Romanies. So how then did I proceed? Before answering this question it is important to stay a little longer with the problems that indwell the classical pattern of Western theological education. However noble, time-honoured and necessary our approach to understanding God may be, however many wonderful tomes may have been written over

---

[54] Luke 15:8-10
[55] Luke 11:41
[56] V.Donovan p.130

the centuries that have edified the faithful, one cannot get away from the fact that in trying to define the ineffable, one runs the grave risk of reducing God to the size of our understanding. In attempting to explain, for example, the dual nature of Christ as both fully God and fully man, or in trying to unravel the mystery of the Trinity, there is always the danger of turning God into a problem we have to try to solve. This process unavoidably reduces God into an object for our critical scrutiny. Meanwhile, sometimes without quite noticing what has happened, we enthrone ourselves as principal subject in the research project. This is what Anselm and the great medieval scholastics would have called "seeking to understand that we might believe."

Something very similar happens within the field of music. As a performer, I was always baffled by the heroic attempts made by academically brilliant musicologists to explain the meaning of a piece of music. As a young musician in my teens I had fallen in love with Schubert's Unfinished Symphony and found the haunting melodies living within me day and night and resonating with my deepest longings. Then, one day, a great act of violence came to pass. My music teacher was at the piano explaining the sonata form of the first movement of Schubert's masterpiece. He came to the point where a wonderful melody emerges within the music in the bass line, appearing almost from another world.

"Here comes the second subject on the cello, lucky fellow."

As my teacher sang these words (very badly) to Schubert's wonderful melody, I felt that he was imposing something ugly and vacuous on the music, robbing it of its profound meaning, a meaning that would be destroyed the moment anyone dared try to explain it in words. He clearly felt that we would have to understand the music first, before we could even hear it. I believed the very opposite. I had to hear the music and take it into my heart, before any kind of "understanding" might be possible.

Within the realm of the divine – and sometime music is divine - we move in and out of understanding; one moment we are seized by wonder, the next we are back in the mundane. We search for ways to bottle our experience. We place a label on the bottle and shelve it carefully, in order to bring it out as and when we feel the need, and ready to administer it to others who, we feel, might benefit from our medicine. Then we are surprised when we discover that their experience of wonder came at a different moment to us and in an entirely different way.

You can't bottle God. He's too big. So how do we even begin to speak of Him? Sometimes, when words and even music fail, it is "the sound of sheer silence" alone that speaks. This is how it was for Elijah at the point of his greatest need when he collapsed in exhaustion on Mount Carmel. God was present neither in the wind, nor the earthquake, nor the fire. [57] God was present in silence. In the absolute absence of any data. This approach to the divine is the ultimate response to a world sick from information overload. When we arrive at the point that we feel another word about God might actually diminish him, we have entered the *apophatic* way. It may look outwardly like a loss of faith. It could, however, be the exact opposite.

Looking back over all my times with the Romanies, I felt that this had been their most precious gift to me. The sheer simplicity of their encounter with God had the effect of carrying me into silence, into a place where I felt that anything I might say by way of commentary might undo what the Holy Spirit was doing within their hearts. All my Christian life hitherto, I had been caught up in the *kataphatic* way. This is the extreme opposite to the way of silence. Here you feel that you can never say enough about God to ever capture who he is. The more words the better! This is a noble tradition that can bear much fruit. But, in the end, this approach can begin to turn against itself. After all, you can never catch the end of the rainbow. It always travels ahead of you. So it is with God. He is the word made flesh, the incarnate Son who becomes real to us through the action of the Holy Spirit. He is fully known to us as the crucified, risen Christ. But he is also the elusive one.

Praise

And so with all these thoughts in mind, with a measure of fear and

---

[57] 1 Kings 19:12 NRSV translation.

trembling, I began my leadership training with the Romanies. This had started on Tuesday evenings in Roy and Pashey's home, where we were joined by Moses, and then flowed over into the Northiam retreat where we were joined by Rachel, Charlotte and Annie. I felt it important that whatever "teaching" I offered should emerge from a sense of already having entered the nearer presence of God. This we did by drawing on our growing repertoire of simple songs. In stark contrast to the traditional Anglican approach, the Romanies were most at ease when the singing was at its most gusty, even gutsy! By now, we found it entirely natural to move as we sang. In some ways, one-liners like "Halle-halle-halle—lu-u-jah" were the most effective in freeing us up into praise. This would then flow into praying for each other in song: "In our hearts, Lord, be magnified..."

Parable

Only then were we ready for a parable. Jesus' preferred method of teaching was to tell a story packed with meaning, often with an open ending or a sting in the tail. In the first generation, these parables were passed by word of mouth through the community of faith and no doubt were distilled into memorable versions easy to pass on. Only when the first generation was beginning to die out were the Gospel accounts of the New Testament written up, in order to keep the message alive for the next generation. Pre-literate communities retain an extraordinary ability to both tell and recall stories and I was certain that this key Romany skill should not be lost at all costs. And so I would read them the story of the Lost Sheep [58] and then invite them to re-tell the story in their own way. Instantly, Moses told a story about a man who had been walking in the woods and lost his dog. After some long searching he came across a group of children who had found the dog, and there was much rejoicing. Pashey told the story of a mother in a supermarket who had lost her child in the store. She had to abandon her shopping and even the other kids to go looking for the lost one who was eventually found. The whole family rejoiced.

---

[58] Luke 15:1-7

When we came to the parable of the Good Samaritan,[59] I explained first how in Jesus' day, the Samaritans were regarded by the Jews as despised aliens from the north. We then developed two contemporary versions of this parable, which were designed to challenge each of our social groupings in Cranbrook. The first parable, which we acted out, featured a Pikey-Romany as the Good Samaritan who came to the rescue of the man who had been beaten up by local *gorgia* thugs and robbed. This would be the parable to challenge the assumption that all Pikey's are bad. The second parable was designed to challenge the Romany assumption, that all *gorgios* are bad, and featured a *gorgia* (me in fact!) as the Good Samaritan, who came to the rescue of the victim.

Learning from the Vine

As the leadership training progressed, I became concerned that I might unintentionally introduce one of the dark accretions of the system of which I was a product. Nothing is more destructive of the Gospel and of genuine community, than the spirit of competition. In its most sinister form, leaders in the church build an identity and even a career on the back of the precious things of God. Vincent Donovan's work with the Masai tribes forced him to confront the shadow side of his own culture:

> "The strange, changing, mobile, temporary, disappearing communities of America can leave one without any experience of what community is. The different groupings there in America do have one common denominator -competition within the group. An individual's worth within any group is pretty much determined by his or her achievements, talents, skill, or beauty. And even if one is talented, it can sometimes be very difficult to be recognized because of the fierceness of competition present. The endowments and talents that are present are often envisaged not as contributions to a community, but as additions to one's personal stature. Such are the bitter-sweet fruits of intense individualism. The concept and reality of the priesthood have to be affected by such an atmosphere". [60]

---

[59] Luke 10:25-37
[60] V. Donovan, p. 141-2

I was horrified at the thought that anything like this might creep into the Romany community. I was reminded of the precious moment when Roy had made his wedding vows, standing empty-handed before Pashey his bride, nothing to give, and yet offering up his whole person as a living sacrifice. If any spirit of competition might find its way into the Romanies, then I felt it would be something they would learn from us. The spirit of individualism, together with its bedfellows of pride and consumerism, were certainly just round the corner, poised ready to erode the sense of community that had been theirs for centuries. To counter this, I introduced early on the New Testament vision of the Body of Christ. We kept coming back to Jesus' metaphor of the Vine. [61] The sap flowing through the branches of the vine is the life-blood of Jesus, flowing through each and every one of us. To belong was to be part of the whole, to fall outside the Vine spelt death. The end product was to bear the fruit of love. I felt a fraud teaching this, for they all understood it a much deeper level than I. However, I carried on unfolding the vision in other ways. Life within the Vine did not have to lead to a bland uniformity for fear of any individual shining too brightly.

Diversity in Unity

Within any flourishing community of faith there would always be a rich diversity of gifts and roles. The five-fold ministries of Apostle, Prophet, Evangelist, Teacher and Pastor[62] were not to be monopolized by a clerical elite, rather they were fundamental charisms given to each and every baptised person. Whilst Jesus had brought each of the five to perfection in his own ministry on earth, we needed to complement each other in order to grow to maturity and become the embodiment of Christ in our context and in our day. We took time to help each other own our individual gifting. I began by asking the group, what they thought my gifting was. Martin is an apostle, one who blazes the trail and pioneers the church of the future. Pashey we then identified as prophet-teacher. Moses is a born evangelist, passionate to bring the good news to others. Charlotte realized that she needed to own her own prophetic gift, as she began to find the courage to share her vision

[61] John 15:1-17
[62] Ephesians 4:11-13

of the burning bush, thus making known the thoughts of God for the encouragement of others. Rachel and Roy we all recognized as pastors, empathic people able to enter into the joys and especially the distress of others. I asked the group what they felt my greatest weakness is. We agreed that it was as pastor. This was an entirely positive thing for the group to own, for it meant that others would need to own and live out this role that, historically, the vicar was presumed to have a monopoly on.

We went on to consider how the first three roles of Apostle, Prophet and Evangelist, could be grouped together as the pioneering ministries. The roles of Teacher and Pastor were the roles needed to sustain the church once it was settled. I shared my view that the historic church had become quite expert in sustaining the settled church but had abandoned the pioneering ministries, under the false assumption that England was still a Christian country. In our new missionary context, we needed to bring alive again the sharp cutting edge of the New Testament church and this was exactly what the Romanies were showing us how to do. For, above all, they had rekindled the role of prophet in our midst. How does God communicate with us? How does he reveal his heart to us? Through those who he gifts with prophetic insight and with the courage to speak out what they believe is on his heart. The burning bush, the heavenly music, the three men swimming: these were all examples of this, and bore witness to a God who still continues to reveal himself to his people as he did in biblical times.

As a means of communicating the five-fold ministry of the church in a memorable way I drew on Life Shapes. [63] The five sides of the pentagon represent these five ministries:

---

[63] The eight Life Shapes were developed by Mike Breen and Bob Hopkins and now form the basis of a Rule of Life for The Order of Mission [TOM], a neo-monastic, international, non-denominational group of disciples, lay and ordained, who seek to lead missional lives in whatever context God has called them. I am a part of TOM.

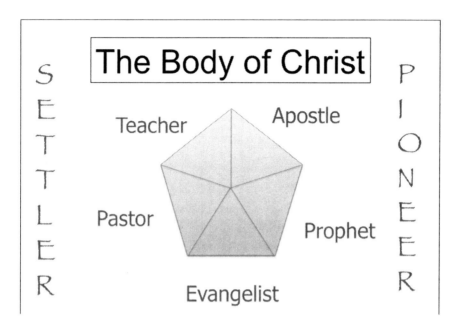

S
E
T
T
L
E
R

The Body of Christ

Teacher

Apostle

Pastor

Prophet

Evangelist

P
I
O
N
E
E
R

Since some of the Romany leaders were not able to read, the use of Life-Shapes proved a way in which they could visually enter into an understanding of the dynamic life of the church. Each life shape proved a helpful aid-memoire, and an easy way of bringing life into what otherwise might have been mere abstractions.

Balancing the three dimensions of life: UP – IN - OUT

We looked together at the three dimensions of our life under God and the need to keep them in a healthy balance. Jesus spent much time alone with his Father and encouraged us to spend time alone in our room in prayer. The UP dimension represents our need to foster a lively relationship with the living Lord. Jesus moved swiftly from time alone with his Father into engagement with his disciples. These times of fellowship were as relaxed as they were intense, as intentional as they were spontaneous. This is the IN dimension of discipleship. How tempting it is, however, to get stuck in the holy huddle and to forget that Jesus moved swiftly on from time invested with the twelve, to passionate engagement with the world, proclaiming the advent of the Kingdom of God, preaching the Good News, healing the sick and driving out the demons. This is the OUT dimension of discipleship. The Holy Spirit guides us to hear the voice of the Father, as we seek to keep a Christ-like balance in all we do both individually and collectively. We agreed that there was a very real danger, as we grew closer to one another in love, that we could become inward looking and lose sight of God's call on our lives to pass on the blessing to others that had been given to us.

Balancing Rest & Work

I had for some time been hoping to find a way of breaking open the whole subject of work with the Romanies. Our retreat provided a good opportunity to look into this delicate area of life. The half-circle that follows represents the rest/work balance that constitutes a healthy life. The pendulum swings back and forth rhythmically on a day-to-day, week to week, month to month basis. God created the world in six days and rested on the seventh. The Sabbath day of rest is a holy day given to the Lord when we are rebuilt spiritually. Adam and Eve were created on the sixth day, and so began their life under God entering a seventh day, a Sabbath day of rest. Thus their working week began with a day of rest. They worked out of rest.

I shared with the Romanies that many *gorgios* in a place like Cranbrook worked extremely hard. We often fell into the trap of collapsing in a heap at the end of a working week with the result that we began to work out of exhaustion, rather than out of rest. I told the Romanies that one of the most precious things I had imbibed from them was what it meant to enter deeply into the Sabbath rest of the Lord. Here, all my chronos-driven work-agendas had no place. Often I would emerge from a time of rest with the Romanies and return to my work refreshed and reinvigorated. For this I was deeply grateful. Then I popped the question. What might the Romanies learn about the rest/work balance from the *gorgios?* At some length we explored the difficulties they are presented with as exiles trying to eke out a living within the alien world of the broader community. Not a few Romanies, they reminded me, were prevented from working on account of health problems. But I pressed on with my challenge and, for the first time, began to address the issue of the Romanies living off the tax that the *gorgios* had paid from their hard-earned wages. I was pleased that we had achieved a level of mutual trust that made the raising of such questions possible.

Following these delicate discussions there arose a fresh determination amongst the able-bodied to seek paid work and, above all, a commitment to the education of their children. Some of those just approaching adulthood renewed their determination to get themselves vocational training and find work. The half-circle proved a helpful tool to capture the rest-work dimension of life:

All Apprentices – All Teachers

Throughout these leadership-training sessions my aim was not so much to impart knowledge as to develop key skills. The sharing of testimonies and the re-telling of parables was the first step. Then, when reviewing what we had learnt in the previous session, I would invite one of the group to explain the last Life-Shape we had looked at. Gradually, I began to hand over the leading of our singing to Pashey and the leading of prayers to others. In this way, I was trying to apprentice others gently into leadership. After the group had seen this pattern in operation for a time, we began to look together at the underlying principles of empowering others to lead. Here the four-sided Life-Shape of the square was helpful.

This pattern is delightfully modelled by Jesus who, no doubt, would have encountered it both in his apprenticeship as a carpenter and from the Rabbis. Once Jesus, aged thirty, begins his public ministry following his baptism and the temptations, we find him beginning to apprentice the twelve disciples whom he had handpicked. At first, we see him simply fleshing out, before their eyes, what ministry in the power of the Spirit looks like. At this stage, the disciples simply observe. They are full of confidence and enthusiasm.

Things get tougher for them when Jesus moves them on to the next stage and invites them to take an active role in sharing the ministry with him. As the disciples turn the corner into the third stage of their apprenticeship, the twelve, and later the seventy-two, are sent out to do the work of the Kingdom. They remain fully accountable to Jesus and are now beginning to learn the ropes through trial and error. Jesus is there to pick up the pieces when things go wrong and to continue to model ministry for them. The final, fourth stage is reached when we find Jesus beginning to call the twelve "friends".[64] For now, at last, they have reached the stage when they can take real initiative themselves and, ultimately, lead the church forward without Jesus there for them in person. By this point, Jesus will have effectively passed on his authority and skills to the Apostles who then, in their turn, will have learnt the skills of indentifying the latent ministries in others, and the imperative of empowering, training and releasing new apprentices to carry forward the Gospel to the next area of mission and the next generation of believers.

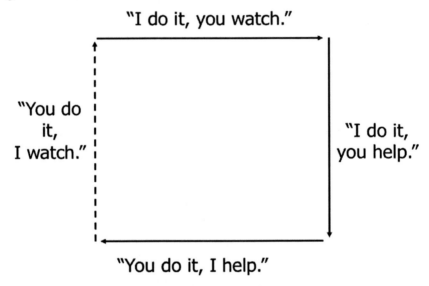

"I do it, you watch."

"You do it, I watch."

"I do it, you help."

"You do it, I help."

By the time Jesus came to return to his Father in heaven, he had developed a group of men and women who knew the very deepest intimacy and love for him and for one another. Yet, amazingly, he had not left them dependent on his ongoing physical presence but was able to rely on them to carry on the same work he had been doing. He even tells them: "Very truly I tell you, all who have faith in me will do the works I have been doing, and they will do even greater things than these, because I am going to the Father."[65]

---

[64] John 15:15 "I no longer call you servants, because servants do not know their master's business. Instead, I have called you friends, for everything that I learned from my Father I have made known to you."
[65] John 14:12

I had been aware of the danger of making all this sound rather abstract and academic. To give it all a real hands-on feel, I had begun by sitting one of the ladies down on a chair and pretending to be an expert hairdresser apprenticing Charlotte. To start with she watched. Then she began to pass me the scissors and other things I needed. When the next client arrived, I allowed her to cut the hair whilst I passed her the kit. Finally, I sat and observed my newly trained colleague. Then I stood up, handed the keys of the business over to Charlotte and invited her to train up Annie, one of her clients who had shown an interest in hairdressing. Some weeks later, I mentioned the square to Charlotte and she instantly remembered all the fun we had had pretending to cut hair. The principles were there!

Towards indigenous leadership

Throughout all my work with the Romanies I was always conscious that they might become too dependent on me, both as one who had become a friend, and as one who made things happen for them. From time to time I would remind them that one day I would no longer be around; the ultimate test of my ministry would be whether what the Lord had built up among us proved sustainable. I found this an extraordinarily difficult thing to communicate and to realize. But, of one further principle I was equally convinced. For this fledgling Romany community of faith to continue to develop and bear fruit, the leadership in its next phase would have to be Romany leadership.

The writings of Rolland Allen and Vincent Donovan, among many others, had long convinced me that the worst possible mistake the church could make when bringing the Gospel into a new culture would be to leave them dependent on "foreign" church structures. This was the classic error that the great missionary movements of modern times had made right up to the 1950s. Indeed, the germ of mono-cultural imperialism is still alive in a most virulent form in some traditional communities. Some who hold authority in the church continue to believe, against all the evidence, that there is only one way of doing church and that is the way they know. For them, there is only one way to achieve unity and that is to insist that things are done in their way. Attempts to enforce unity in this fashion always result in the killing of creativity and the death of the very diversity that is the by-product of that creativity. But God cannot be systematically forced into a cultural straightjacket. His response is always the same: he slips out and moves on. And so do the people who are thirsty for him.

The French Romany Revival

The story of the revival of faith in the Romany communities across the world has a great deal to teach us here. It is widely believed that the initial spark came in 1950 in the French town of Lisieux[66]. The story goes that Zino, a young Romany father, was dying in the local hospital of an intestinal peritonitis.[67] His extended family was so overcome with distress that they were unable to leave the hospital. In the end their wailing was more than the hospital staff were able to cope with and they had to leave. Shortly afterwards, Madame Duvil, the young man's mother, discovered an evangelical tract in her handbag that she had put there some months earlier and forgotten about. A woman in a local shop was able to read the tract and explain, that it had been produced by a local Pentecostal church. Madame Duvil headed straight for the church and burst in on the minister as he was in full flow preaching. "My son is dying. Come and pray for him!" The minister responded, "Your son will not die. God can do anything and he'll give him back to you. Where is he? We'll go and lay hands on him." They headed straight for the hospital where the medical team allowed them to enter the room where Zino was dying. A little later, during a routine examination, a doctor was startled to discover that the young man's fever was passing. Before long, the medical team realized that he had been healed.

News of the miracle spread through the family, but it was not until 1952 that the real spiritual awakening happened. Contact was made with a non-Romany *Assemblies of God* minister, one Clement le Cossec. Members of the family were baptised first in the Holy Spirit and then by full immersion in the sea at St Marc, on the outskirts of Brest. Some of them had longed for

---

[66] Lisieux is well known as a centre of Carmelite spirituality. St Therese de Lisieux was a Roman Catholic Carmelite nun who was born in 1877.
The story of this healing is recorded in "Travelling Home", Joe Ridholls 1986
[67] This story is especially poignant for me. In 1965 my older brother, Stephen, aged fifteen, died in hospital in France following a two week battle with the same condition.

years to receive Holy Communion but this had been denied them, because their partnerships were not regarded by the Roman Catholic Church as proper marriages. In due course, Le Cossec arranged for them to be legally married. The revival then spread swiftly through Romany communities across France, the *Assemblies of God* and Le Cossec playing a critical role throughout. They had the insight to realize that the new Romany communities of faith that were springing up should be supported in every way possible, but fully empowered to develop church in the way that was appropriate to Romany culture. Le Cossec understood from the outset, that the key to sustaining the revival was to apprentice indigenous Romany preachers. Any attempt to impose pre-existing patterns on the Romanies would to drain the life-blood out of what God was clearly doing.

Rolland Allen, writing in the early twentieth century and addressing the mission to the "natives" of India and China, makes the same point. It is not difficult to see why his writings have been most popular amongst Pentecostals.

"…those to whom we minister the Spirit
can only show forth His power in their own spontaneous activity.
Action done under compulsion or direction is no revelation of the Spirit.
If we want to see what is the character of any living thing,
we must see what it does in free conditions…

If we want to see the manifestation of the Spirit
in a form which can be understood,
it must be in the unfettered activity of Christians
under their own natural conditions."

"It is here that we see the importance of the establishment of little native churches
which are obviously and unmistakably not under our control,
but fully equipped with their own ministers
and possessing full spiritual authority to direct their own life.
We should spend our strength establishing as many of these as possible." [68]

---

[68] Rolland Allen [1868-1947] *"The Ministry of the Spirit" Selected Writings edited by David M. Paton 2006. Chapter 3 "Mission Activities Considered in Relation to the*

It was just this kind of freedom that the new Romany communities of faith enjoyed as the revival spread, first across France and then into many other countries. Le Cossec formed the movement *"Vie et Lumiere"* (Life and Light) and the growth continues to this day.

A Romany Creed

It was with these principles of indigenous, autonomous leadership in mind that I set about getting the Romanies to write their own creed. The opportunity came when we were on our three-day retreat at Northiam. I set the scene like this:

> "I want you to imagine that you are travelling into a new country that has lots of Romanies in it. But they are Romanies who have not yet heard anything at all about Jesus. You're on the move and you've only got a little time to explain your faith to them. What do you say? What do they really need to know? What is not so important and what is actually unhelpful? Think for a moment about how you would describe what a car is to someone who's never seen one before. What's more important, the colour of the seats or the fact that it's got a steering wheel? In the same way, ask yourselves, what is it about your faith in Jesus that has made all the difference to your lives."

I set up two groups, each with its own scribe and a large sheet of paper on which to record ideas. I found it fascinating to see what emerged over the hour that followed. It was a huge encouragement for me to see how many of the things we had shared, experienced and valued over the months had been retained and owned. When we all came together, I pointed out one or two areas of the faith that they had not included, asking them whether, for example, they felt baptism was important to mention. I resisted the temptation to impose any kind of formal systematic framework on their emerging creed. It had to be theirs and theirs alone to have any real authenticity. Only this way would there

---

Manifestation of the Spirit". p.111-2

be any sense of ownership and any possibility of the creed being used to keep alive and pass on the faith they had discovered. The only thing I imposed on their creed was standard grammar and spelling. This I did, so that it would be accessible to *gorgios* and be taken seriously by them.

As Pashey dictated to me the creed they had written and I typed it up on my laptop, I was struck by the flow of thought. It had none of the formulaic structure of the historic creeds, which had been drawn up by highly trained theologians in the early centuries to address the heresies of the day. Rather, this Romany creed flowed like the words of a psalm, where rapid changes of focus are quite normal and indeed reflect more closely the way we think when in deep meditative prayer. There was something delightfully Johannine about these simple, short clauses, all centering around the living presence of Jesus. He is for them not an inspiring concept or ethical ideal. Rather he is "a running stream" that flows even through the desert, "a candle" that cannot be blown out.

As you will see below, I have followed the pattern of New Testament Greek and introduced no punctuation. This allows one phrase to flow seamlessly into the next, like ripples on the surface of living water. The aim is not formal closure on propositional statements of faith. This creed weaves itself into the fabric of the whole of life...

We believe

Jesus love is like a running stream

Flowing to all corners of the world

It flows high and it flows low

It reaches everywhere

Even to the desert

Jesus died for our sins

He is our Lord and saviour

And the only way to eternal life

We believe

The Father sent his only Son

To die for our sins

And we believe Jesus rose on the third day

And we believe there is life after death

Because Jesus conquered death

We believe

When you open your heart to Jesus

You will receive the Holy Spirit

Jesus will be with you every day

Good or bad

Keep your faith

Accept the Son

And you will accept the Father

And the Father will accept you

The Father lives inside the Son

The Son lives in the Father

We live in Jesus

And Jesus lives in us

Don't matter what you've got

Or what you are

Jesus always loves you

And always welcomes you with open arms

You are nothing without Jesus in your life

Because you are not fulfilled without him

Accept Jesus as your Lord and saviour

There is nothing on earth better than being saved

And being re-born

And put into a new life with Christ

The best thing anyone can do

Is to be baptised into the name of Jesus

You have a new life

Your sin is gone away

The old is gone

And the new life begins

Following the truth

Of a living person

The way the truth and the life

When you find the treasure in your heart

You want to find others and tell them

To tell them the good news

That there is light even in the darkest places

We were lost and now we have been found

We were in the dark and now we are in the light

Jesus can turn your life around

Don't matter what you've done

Your heavenly Father loves you

Because he sent his only Son to save us

When you come to God empty handed

Weak and vulnerable

God is then able to fill us and make us strong

Don't believe in your own way

Gather with others to have fellowship

To remember Jesus

And what he came here for

When you gather together in fellowship

The vine grows stronger

But when you cut yourself off

You die

In the same way, you get lost in darkness

Jesus is like a candle

Shining in the darkest places

There is no storm and no wind

that can blow the candle out

it only gets brighter

Black can cover anything

But it can't cover the light of the world

We all have different gifts

That we all use in different ways

Come to your Lord with a joyful heart

Be open

Be as a child

Asking your Father

And your Father will give to you

Be attentive

Listen to what is being said to you

And he will surely lead you the holy way

We believe that there are two ways to choose from.

One leads to life

And the other leads to death

The road that leads to life is the narrow way of Jesus Christ

God's love is so high you can't get over it

So low you can't get under it

So wide you can't get round it

Put all these things together and it makes a cross

The cross of Jesus

Jesus told us to make disciples of all people on earth

Baptising them in the name of the Father, the Son and the

Holy Spirit

We break the bread and drink the wine

To share with one another

The remembrance of Jesus Christ

It is the bread of life to eternal life

And the wine is his blood shed for us

We believe Jesus is coming back.

Praise the Lord and Hallelujah

He is coming to judge the living and the dead

And to make a new heaven and a new earth

To claim his victory

All of his people

Love and respect your neighbour

As you would like your neighbour to love and respect you

We are learning to love and forgive our enemies

As God loves and forgives us all

All things in this world

God created

The heavens and the earth

You and me

Amen

What happened next, following the typing up of this Romany Creed, will always stay with me; it was the most precious thing to have come out of our retreat at the Northiam Oasts. I went over to Sarah White's office and asked her if she could print out the creed for me. When I came back to the main building a little later I handed the copy, hot off the press, to Pashey. "Look Pashey," I said "I'll take your kids and baby-sit them downstairs for half an hour or so. This'll give you a chance to set the creed to music if you like." Something in me told me she would be able to perform this – humanly speaking - impossible feat. I gave Pashey my recording device, showed her how it worked, and took little Derby and Reuben off her hands. Thirty minutes later, she came downstairs and handed me back the recording device as though she'd come back from a nap. In fact, as Pashey told me later, she had gone upstairs to the sitting room where we had earlier conceived the words of the creed, looked out the window for a little and prayed for inspiration. Then she had turned on the recording device and simply began to sing the words of the creed.

It was not until later that day, when I was driving home to Cranbrook, that I had a chance to put on my earphones and listen to the recording. It was simply the most beautiful piece of spontaneous and effortless music making that I had ever heard. The only way I can describe the style of singing is to say that it is a kind of contemporary folk-jazz-gospel equivalent of plainchant! With amazing poise Pashey had transformed the words of the creed into a timeless, passionate river of praise. By the time it came to the end, Martin had become very emotionable indeed and was having some difficulty seeing the road ahead of him. But I was still only half way home and the performance had not yet finished. For as I drove slowly into Hawkhurst and approached the lights, to my utter astonishment, a *second* setting of the creed began to unfold in a fresh, more flowing style, and in a new tonality.

As I drove on slowly to Cranbrook, I found myself asking, "how is it possible, that a mother of five boys all under ten, who only began her schooling when aged 10 and who had received no formal training in music, could spontaneously produce two musical settings of a creed within thirty minutes?! And this was a creed that takes seven minutes to read and over twenty minutes to sing twice through!"

Picasso once encountered a similar gift in the artwork of a Romany-Spanish girl. He praised what he called her shining naïf style and found himself asking the same question I was asking: "how can it be possible that a Gipsy girl without studies expresses such a sensibility and colours in her paintings..."[69] Though I am not sure that Picasso would agree, I concluded for myself that, whilst I might have no way of explaining in human terms what Pashey had achieved, for God "all things are possible". Filled with the Holy Spirit, she had breathed the words on the printed page into song in a way reminiscent of Aslan, who sang creation into being in C.S Lewis's Narnia stories.

---

[69] *Micaela Flores Amaya, "La Chunga"* (Marseille, 1938)
Even though "La Chunga" is known worldwide as a Flamenco dancer (and Flamenco artists are not included in this webpage) her mention here is as a Romany painter. Grown-up in Barcelona, she was first a talented dancer since her childhood and later she began to paint by spontaneous inspiration. Her "shining naïf" style was praised by Picasso, who said of her: "How can it be possible that a Gipsy girl without studies expresses such a sensibility and colours in her paintings...". She has also featured as a cinema actress. She has been awarded the Golden Medal of the Fine Arts Circle of Madrid, and other prizes.

The Romany Lord's Prayer

There was one other piece of creative work that we undertook whilst away together on retreat at Northiam. Recognizing that the Romanies have their language, which they speak when there are no *gorgios* around, I thought it would be both fun, and potentially rewarding, for them to translate the Lord's Prayer into their own language. Whilst the grammatical base they use is clearly English, much of the vocabulary is their own, some words having their roots - so it is believed - in Hindi. Many of the words of their Anglo-Romany might well be understood by Romanies from other countries.

The translation work was not easy for us and it became clear to me that there is no agreed vocabulary amongst the different families and that, for a variety of reasons, their linguistic heritage is under threat. However, we had a great deal of fun together and produced the following which we now use at our Friday Cluster gatherings...

Our Father in Heaven
Our Da up a koi

Hallowed be your name
Cushti yer nav

Your Kingdom come
Yer Folky will kur

Your will be done
Yer will kur

On earth as it is in heaven
Down a doie as e-jowld up a kye

Give us today our daily bread
Jazz us some panem

And forgive us our sins
And forgive us for what we kurred was wrong

As we forgive those who sin against us
As we forgive the folky for what they kur agin us

And lead us not into temptation
And don't jess us to the Mullah

But deliver us from evil
But kurr us away from the Mullah

For yours is the Kingdom, the power and the glory
For yours is the Folky, the Poke and the Koch

For ever and ever
Dordy, dordy, dordy,

Amen!
a geries!

Chapter twenty-six

Unity & Diversity

"I have given them the glory that you gave me,
that they may be one as we are one-
I in them and you in me-
so that they may be brought to complete unity.
Then the world will know that you sent me
and have loved them even as you have loved me."[70]

Jesus' prayer to the Father shortly before his passion makes clear that he placed the very highest value on unity. As he and the Father are one, so Jesus' disciples on earth were to remain one after his return to the Father. A unified church would be a sign to the world that God is alive. The church was in fact a single, united body of believers from the moment Jesus left earth until the outpouring of the Holy Spirit at Pentecost. Indeed, the church remained united right up until the point that the Gospel was taken beyond the land of the Jews. The very earliest expression of church was, therefore, of a fully united band of believers who shared everything in common and who were held in high regard by the broader community.[71] They were, however, right up to that point, a culturally homogenous group of Jews. Had they remained such, the embryonic church would have fizzled out within a generation. The real challenge came when the Jewish Christians were forced to leave Jerusalem for their own safety following the martyrdom of Stephen.

As they spread out into Palestine and on into the Greek-speaking world, they brought with them the Gospel and, empowered by the Holy Spirit, took the first steps towards fulfilling the mandate Jesus had given them to bring the Good News of the Kingdom of God to every ethnic group on earth. The gentiles embraced the Gospel and new churches began to spring up as the Apostles carried the mission forward. These new communities of faith co-existed alongside the

---

[70] John 17:22-23
[71] Acts 2:42-47; 4:32-35

Jewish Synagogues where the Gospel had received a mixed welcome. Significant tensions quickly arose between the Jewish and the gentile Christians and it wasn't until the Council of Jerusalem in c.AD 50 that the way forward became clear. The decision made by the Apostles at the council was absolutely crucial to the survival of the church. Everyone could see that the new gentile believers were clearly full of the Spirit. There was, therefore, no way they should have to submit to all the Laws of Moses, rather they would be guided by the indwelling Spirit to live lives pleasing to God.

The decision of the Council opened the floodgates. Irrespective of their cultural background and ethnicity, the new converts were free to express their faith within their own culture.[72] Whilst certain practices and attitudes from their pagan pasts would have to go, no other group could impose their own patterns of living the Christian life on any other group. Unity was still paramount. But unity could only ever be achieved through the active encouragement of an ever-greater diversity. As the Gospel was absorbed by each new community, so the Holy Spirit enabled them to express their new life in Christ within the terms of their own culture. Only in this way could the Gospel be taken to the ends of the earth and act like yeast within every people group, affirming the good, challenging the bad, and so bringing about the Kingdom of God on earth.

Today, many of us would say that, whenever a group of people come to faith in Christ and begin to share their lives with one another, a "fresh expression" of church has come to birth. The emergence of the New Testament Church from within the traditions of Judaism was the first "fresh expression" of church. Two thousand years of church history tell the story of how the Gospel continued to find fresh expression within each new people group as the core message was lived out in ways appropriate and relevant to each culture. The church of Jesus Christ proved infinitely adaptable to each new context in a way, which no other world religion has matched. However, as each fresh expression of church emerged from within the inheritance of the past, the question of how to maintain unity was never far away. Jesus himself had made

---

[72] See Acts 15

it clear that the new wine of the Kingdom should not be forced into old wine skins, nor the old cloth patched with the new. Paul knew only too well how precarious was the process of transmitting the Gospel to the next generation. He described it as "the birth pangs of the new creation." [73]

The extraordinary story of the fresh awakening of faith amongst the Romany people of Cranbrook is part of this unfolding story of salvation history. Watching the new baby come to birth has been for me as great a joy as witnessing the birth of my own three children, Rebecca, Naomi and Leo. Being caught up in the whole process of new birth, whether of my children or in the birth of new communities of faith, has been the greatest privilege of my life. Much of the time, I have found myself having to learn how to be a midwife, discovering how to share in the joys and the agonies of the birth process, how to help without getting in the way, how to release, rather than control. Many, these days, refer to this approach to ministry as "watching what God is doing and joining in". It has more to do with the opening of eyes and ears and waiting, than with carefully constructed five year plans. My work with the Romanies has been about learning how to immerse myself in an utterly new culture before daring to do anything, about being willing to be changed before expecting anyone else to change. It has been about learning to be flexible and adaptable to seeing things in entirely new ways, about being open to the changing needs of every moment. At my ordination service I was asked to do something like this when I had to promise to "proclaim the faith afresh" in my generation.

Our Diocesan Missioner for Fresh Expressions of Church, Kerry Thorpe, joined us at one of our Friday evening cluster meetings and commented to me at the end: "This is a Fresh Expression of church!" If something like the Romany awakening of faith had happened ten years earlier, there would have been very little in place within the structures of the Church of England to affirm and own the emergence of a gypsy gathering of believers in church buildings. And so we rejoice that what has happened here in Cranbrook in recent times is understood now as an authentic, Anglican missional movement and expression of the

---

[73] Romans 8:32

historic faith. Indeed, my reflection on these times and the writing of this book has only been possible thanks to the three months' sabbatical that the Bishops granted me.

Jesus promised us that he would build his church and that "the gates of hell would not prevail against it". [74] Clearly, he is doing so. But he also prayed that we should be one, as he and his Father are one. Jesus is as passionate about the unity of his church as he is about its growth. Unity and diversity are, for Jesus, two sides of the same coin. Diversity must never be at the expense of unity; unity must never be at the expense of diversity.

With all this in mind, I believe we all need to ask certain questions of ourselves. Firstly, our local, Romany fresh expression of church needs to ask of itself:

"Do we honour the tradition from which our new life has sprung?"

"How will we, as a new gathering of believers, continue to belong to the life of the church as a whole?"

"In what ways will we contribute to and enhance the life of the church as a whole?"

Secondly, our inherited church, which has provided ministry and premises for the new gathering, needs to ask of itself:

"Do we understand ourselves as mother church to this fledgling community of faith, as the rock from which they were cut and the quarry from which they were hewn?[75]

"Do we fully affirm and own the cultural distinctiveness of this fresh expression of church?"

---

[74] Matthew 16:18
[75] Isaiah 51:1

"Will we continue to support this movement of the Holy Spirit in every way we can, understanding it as part of the *misseo dei*, the mission of God?"

I see three possible ways forward, whenever a fresh expression of church emerges alongside the inherited church. The first two ways I believe are wrong. The third I hope is a potentially fruitful way forward.

The first approach amounts to schism. It is the full separation of the two forms through a mutual failure to hold the new and the old together creatively. Tragically, this is what happened in the early church, when the gentile church and Jewish church were not able to sustain creative co-existence into the second century. The Jewish church rapidly atrophied and died, whilst the gentile church continued to flourish...

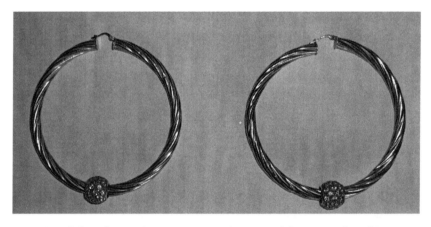

Tradition & Fresh Expression distanced from each other.

The second approach is the attempt to achieve unity by collapsing the two forms into one another. But unity can never be achieved by attempting to enforce uniformity. This was the classic mistake of many of the great missionary movements through the centuries. Rolland Allen captures the mindset perfectly in an imaginary dialogue between an old-school missionary and a fresh thinker. The former says to the latter:

"It is all very well to believe in Christ; we all do that;
but to say that Africans can do without control from us, that is going
to far.

Didn't I tell you long ago that we are sent to control, and control we must!" [76]

We may laugh at the way our colonialist forebears went about their missions. But the legacy lives on. One prominent church leader here in Cranbrook said that the only way to achieve unity is for the Romanies to be taught to read in order that they can then recite the liturgy together with everyone else. However well intentioned this may be, it is in truth mono-cultural imperialism of the worst sort. No one in their right mind would suggest that the way to achieve unity would be for everyone to throw away their liturgies and worship the Romany way. Any kind of imperialism, any attempt to force unity, is fundamentally opposed to the spirit of freedom, flexibility, and diversity that pervades the New Testament church. At various times in Anglican history the church has attempted, both at home and abroad, to engineer unity through the legal enforcement of a monochrome uniformity. What you end up with is a grey sky in which all distinctiveness and creativity is eliminated. This approach might be represented thus...

Tradition & Fresh Expression collapsed into one another.

---

[76] Rolland Allen, *St Paul and the Judaisers: A Dialogue, p 117-127*

But there is a third way forward. Here you see circles overlapping. They happen to be Romany earrings!

Tradition & Fresh Expression overlapping.

This approach allows each tradition to freely develop its own distinctive life and mission. There is a part of each circle that stands on its own. At the same time, each circle overlaps with the other; this represents the times when the two communities come to share together with one another. The overlap represents the place where the tension must be held, where the opportunity comes to encounter the other who is different. This is the place where all are challenged to lay down their own agendas in a desire to grow together through a reciprocal exchange of cultures. At worst, the tension becomes unbearable and unsustainable. At best, the cross-fertilization creates a synergy in which the total becomes greater than the sum of the parts. Here, the interface of different cultures gives birth to creativity and mutual delight. This represents, for me, a dimension of the Kingdom of God fully realized. I have had many glimpses of it, but suspect that the best wine will only come at the end – in heaven.

One lovely foretaste must have been at the wedding at Cana, where the wine that Jesus had created from water was at once new wine only seconds old, *and* the most mature wine ever tasted! Here the old and the new are not so much mixed together to achieve a compromise - a kind of nice Anglican *via media* - rather as the new and the old come together, something entirely new and completely unexpected begins to take shape. This is the wine of the Kingdom that I taste when hearing the music of J.S Bach. For he was able to take the traditions of his day and so infuse them with fresh, sparkling creativity, that the open minded listener is transported into another world that they had hitherto only dreamed of. This is the music of the Gospels.

Jesus came to earth to open all our senses to glimpse an entirely new way for humans to be together. This would be a place where all the dividing walls that separate us would fall away as we discover our identities in Christ alone. In the New Testament church, this meant that the walls separating Jew and Gentile, slave and free, male and female would no longer be of any importance.[77] In our context here in Cranbrook, this would mean that the distinction between Romany and *gorgia* would be enriching, rather that divisive. This is the music of the church that Jesus promised he would continue to build here on earth.

---

[77] Galatians 3:28

Lottie & a resident from Hillside, a home for vulnerable adults

I would wish to go a step further and say that, if we want to understand the Gospel at all, then we have to set aside all our pre-conceived ideas and simply observe the effervescent divine chemistry at work within any authentic community of faith. As Bishop Leslie Newbigin famously put it:

> "…the only hermeneutic of the gospel,
> is a congregation of men and women
> who believe it and live by it." [78]

This is the ideal. However, I have come to understand that not all have grown to that point of maturity that they are able to lay hold of this vision. Life in the overlap, life in the intersection between the two circles, is simply too painful and too distressing for many to bear. I am reminded of how the music of masters like Bach was inaccessible to most of the clergy of his day. People cannot be taken into life in the

---

[78] Leslie Newbigin, *The Gospel in a Pluralistic Society* p.227

overlap against their will. Growth towards maturity comes only when a group of people feel sufficiently held within the familiar, that they feel ready to venture into the unknown.

Afghan, Romany & Gorgia
Zaman, Roy, Lee, Ephraim, Ben

And so, at St Dunstan's, we developed an approach which sets people free to be themselves within their own cultural group and to come together with others on the many occasions we create for them. Archbishop Rowan Williams has called this a *"mixed economy"* approach. Initially, we applied this to our Sunday pattern of worship where three distinct tracks of worship were created - 8.00am Book of Common Prayer; 9.30am Choral Eucharist/Mattins, 11.15am Contemporary Praise Service. Then we applied the same principle to our mid-week gatherings where each cell group represents different groupings within the broader church family. And, most significantly, this principle we applied with the new Romany community, who met with me every Friday evening as a Cluster, but who also gather together with others for the 11.15 Sunday service and together with the broader church community for other services and events. Sustaining a *mixed economy* under the roof of one single parish church in the small town of Cranbrook stretches us all to the limit -sometimes beyond the limit. But would anything less bring us closer to unity? Would anything less advance the Kingdom of God on earth?

The picture of the two overlapping circles offers a way forward that is realistic and dynamic. It offers a way in which radically different cultural groups can express their faith in Christ in their own unique ways, yet still experience what it means to be one single, universal body of believers. This is clearly the vision at the heart of that round-robin letter directed to all the churches around Ephesus:

> "There is one body and one Spirit,
> just as you were called to one hope when you were called;
> one Lord, one faith, one baptism;
> one God and Father of all,
> who is over all and through all and in all." [79]

Vincent Donovan comments:

> "Every artificial attempt from the time of the Tower of Babel, up to the United nations to "make a great people, a people which is one," has failed. I believe that only Christianity has the inherent capability to accomplish this, the inner strength necessary to match the primeval force of racism and tribalism."[80]

---

[79] Ephesians 4:4-6
[80] Vincent J. Donovan – *Christianity Rediscovered – An Epistle from the Masai 1978, 1982* pages 52-53

Chapter twenty-seven

A time to stay – A time to move on

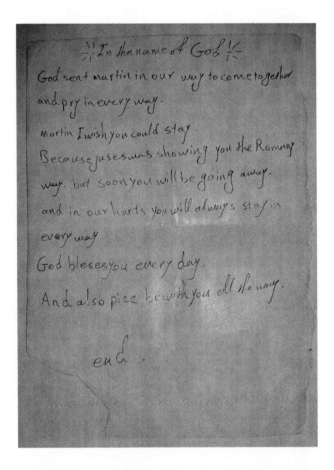

"In the name of God!
God sent martin in our way to come together
and pry in every way.
Martin I wish you could stay.
Because jusesus was showing you the Romany
way. but soon you will be going away.
and in our harts you will always stay in
every way.
God blesesyou every day.
And also pice be with you all the way.

end.

For a variety of reasons it became clear to my wife, Margareta and I that the time had come for us to move on to new pastures. We reached this decision in the summer of 2008, at the very height of the Romany awakening. It is not the purpose of this book to explore the darker side of why a move had become necessary; the reader will perhaps have read a little between the lines of this narrative and understood something of the rising tensions within the parish.

At a personal level, I was simply torn apart at the prospect of leaving these dear people whom the Lord had touched so deeply. They had taken me to their heart, rescued me from a situation that had become almost intolerable and adopted me as one of their own into their extended family of over fifty. The prayer above was written by Charlotte, eighteen years old at the time. It captures, in its utter simplicity, the feelings we share, weaves them into the faith we share, and so makes sense of what was happening. However painful the break may be, Jesus is there at the centre of it and he will continue to unfold his will and his way to us as we all move on into the future he has prepared for us.

As I began to look around for a new post, I set a Gideon-like fleece before the Lord.[81] I needed Him to make His will absolutely clear if I were to move on in the right spirit and understand what had happened as part of His will. It came as quite a surprise that the second and third applications I submitted were followed swiftly by invitations to interview. I had thought that, at fifty-seven years of age, I might have passed my sell-by date and that the move might not happen for some time, if at all.

The second interview was for the vacancy at Christchurch, Bushmead, Luton. Throughout the day I prayed "Lord, if you do not want me to get this job, that is fine with me. I'll just stay and continue my work with the Romanies. If, however you do want me to get this job, then that's fine too. May your will be done, not mine."

And so it was with a spirit of openness that I entered the excellent process the parish had set up. Although I was in torment about the possibility of having to leave behind all that had happened with the Romanies, this torment was eclipsed by an unspeakable and almost over-whelming joy. For I was carrying around in my heart an experience of love that had, within a short space of time, completely changed my understanding of life and of ministry. Charlotte's prayer gets it perfectly: "Jesus was showing you the Romany way". This most excellent way was something I could take anywhere with me, and which even the gates of hell could not rob me of. I felt swept along by this and carried through the day of the interview. Paradoxically, it could just be that the very thing I was so clinging to was the same thing that had brought about the invitation

---

[81] Judges 6:37-39

to take the post in Luton. In not a few ways, the good people there had made it clear to me that they would welcome a leader who would have a heart for the marginalized and the vilified people of their town.

God bless you, dear Romanies,
for maybe it is you who are responsible for bringing about my move!

The day the announcement was made at St Dunstan's that Margareta, Leo and I were to move on was extremely 'emotionable'. The news came as a complete shock to the Romanies and left them deeply perplexed at first. In my last sermon I broke open Jesus' parable of the "six acts of mercy"[82]. Towards the end I spoke of a turning point in my nine years of ministry at St Dunstan's, when I had begun to search out a fresh way of understanding the Gospel in the hope that it would inform how I should live out my ministry…

> "… I began to take the words of today's Gospel literally and ask the King to lead me to the most needy in the community, in the hope that I might somewhere be of use to Him – perhaps also in the hope that I might even find Him somewhere out there. Where were Cranbrook's equivalent of the naked, hungry and thirsty, those who needed clothing, feeding and watering? Where were the sick, the prisoners and the resident aliens who needed healing, visiting and welcoming? It is very hard to feed a mouth that is already full, and a heart that is already satisfied. But when I found myself, within the space of a few months from beginning the search, standing before a huge nest of little birds all screaming out for spiritual food and nurture because they have been marginalized for 600 years then, suddenly, I found myself back in business. And, of course, the King was already there when I arrived. A powerful, unseen presence, feeling all the pain of rejection and vilification as though it were his own, and entering deeply into all the resultant dysfunction, isolation, and tribalism. Since August 31 over forty of these of who I am speaking have asked for baptism and received it, amongst them several Afghan boys running for their lives.

---

[82] Matthew 25:31-end.

Margaret Brearley said this: "The treatment of Romany Gypsies has become the litmus test for a humane society." The litmus test of St Dunstan's at this point in our history is this: will we welcome the Romanies into our church as though, in welcoming them, we are welcoming Jesus himself? This is the sting in the tail of today's Gospel. The King is on the move. Do we have the eyes to see what he is doing? And will we join in? On Friday night, Church House was too small for the fifty Romanies who came along this week. Do we have room for them in our inn? Do we have room for them in the inn of our hearts? I pray we will".

I had been concerned that the Romanies would be able to follow this train of thought, but at several points in the long sermon I was aware that they were with me. At the point when I began to draw them into the picture, spontaneous applause broke out at the 11.15 service. The applause was absolutely not for me. Heaven forbid. Nor was it for the Romanies. It was for the Lord and for what he had done and was continuing to do in our midst. Over the following weeks an important question began to formulate within the Romany community:

Martin accepted us. So we accepted him and his church.
It has become our church.
Now Martin has had to go. Was this because of us?
If so, where does this leave us?

Chapter twenty-eight

Leaving and Empowering

As the reality of our impending move to Luton came home to us, I began to understand more fully what God was up to and to make sense of it in my own heart. My ministry with the Romanies had had an important apostolic dimension to it; I had stepped out into the unknown with a view to bringing the Gospel to a discrete group of people. As the underlying meaning of the word *apostle* suggests, I had been *sent* by God to do this. If I were to remain with the same people indefinitely, my ministry with them would move gradually from being *apostolic* to *pastoral.* I had, in fact, already become aware of this shift in emphasis. Alongside this, I was increasingly conscious that, for these people to come to maturity in faith, and to begin to stand more fully on their own feet as a fresh expression of church, they would need to grow their own leaders from their own people. The leadership-training programme that I had set up from September 2008 had just this in mind. By then, they had understood that I would be moving on and that, at one level this had to happen in order for them to come of age as a new community of faith. With all this in mind, discussions were well underway with Diocesan officials and educators with regard to the formal recognition of the Romany leaders I had been working with, in the hope that they could take over the leadership of the Friday cluster following my imminent departure.

Rolland Allen explores, in depth, the imperative for the missionary to move on having brought the Gospel to a new people group. The failure of the old missionary method was precisely the failure to empower indigenous leaders, thus keeping the people in a dependency culture. Vincent Donovan builds further on this, explaining how he felt impelled to leave each newly converted Masai clan, once they had come to faith. To stay would prevent them ever learning how to express their new faith within the terms of their own culture. The principle is found it its perfect form in Jesus' own ministry. The three years of apprenticeship the disciples enjoyed with their master Rabbi was aimed at empowering them to become apostles at the point when Jesus would leave them.

Indeed, unless he left, the Holy Spirit would not come. They would remain forever milk-babies, dependant on Jesus. The Apostle Paul clearly grasped the same principle at a deep level. Rolland Allen points out how Paul generally moved on after as little as three to four months in a place. Moving on was a vital part in empowering the fragile, newly birthed church to begin to take responsibility for its own internal life and to develop its own distinctive mission. Failure to move on would also have had the effect of terminating Paul's own work as an apostle.

The principle of leaving in order to empower, helped us make sense of my impending move and brought a new dynamic into the work. The three-month sabbatical that I had been granted was giving me space to let go of my role as vicar and to work much more closely with the four key Romany families whose journey of faith continued, as the writing of this book proceeded. At several points, my lack of faith caused me to fear that I was writing an account of a story that was about to run into the sand. But, again and again, I saw the Holy Spirit bring fresh life and vitality into this fragile, vulnerable little community, and always in quite unexpected ways. I began to notice, for example, how the faith of the parents was beginning to percolate down into the lives of their children. Giggly girls were renouncing their smoking, taking seriously the need to get a training and find a job, and beginning to take a lead in the spiritual life of the community. From standing on the edge looking in, they were now singing with ever greater gusto and joining in the prayer for those who were sick or in need from their number. And I rejoiced in the fact that they never stopped laughing.

Roy

Little Roy, aged ten, continued to amaze us with his prophetic insight. One Friday evening, he announced that he had something to say. He then proceeded to tell us all that, whilst many people could read and write very well, it could just be that those who didn't have these skills might able to get closer to God as a direct result of their limitations. I think Jesus would have responded: "I praise you, Father, Lord of heaven and earth, because you have hidden these things from the wise and learned and revealed them to little children. Yes, Father, for this was your good pleasure."[83] Meanwhile, Roy's mother, Pashey, was establishing a foot in the Cranbrook Community Group and bringing an awareness of the Romany dimension into every section of the town's life, even making an impromptu appearance with one of her songs at the end of one of the Friend's lunchtime classical music concerts.

My reading of Rolland Allen sparked another key question that faced us. Allen's thesis was that Paul's missions across the four Roman provinces of Galatia, Achaia, Asia and Macedonia had met with such astonishing success for three core reasons. Firstly, it was a mission directed by the Holy Spirit, not humans. It had not been about God being invited to join in with what humans were doing, but the exact reverse. Indeed, every set back was interpreted by the Apostles as a God-given opportunity. Secondly, Paul maintained a strict discipline of moving on once a new church was established.

I believe that, in my work with the Romanies, I was doing my best to follow these two principles. But Allen drew my attention to a third core reason for Paul's success. Paul had continued to share in the life and mission of each of his churches *even after he had moved on.* The reason I had missed this was easy to see. As an Anglican I was steeped in the historic principle that, once a vicar moves on, he severs all further pastoral contact with people whose faith he has nurtured. There are very sound reasons why this practice has been honoured through the centuries: nothing is worse for an incoming leader than his predecessor still breathing down his neck. However, I began to wonder whether the church might have missed something important in its strict adherence to time-honoured protocol.

---

[83] Luke 10:21

146

At a pastoral level, the prospect of never seeing my Romany friends again seemed inhuman and, for all of us, almost too much to bear. We all recognized that all relationships on earth were transitory and I shared with them Luke's moving account of Paul's final meeting with the Ephesian elders before he embarked on his long and final journey towards what must surely have been his martyrdom[84]. However, one of the key reasons for the amazing multiplication of little communities of faith in and around Ephesus had been Paul's keenness to maintain pastoral contact with them in the early stages of their development, through letters and occasional visits. This went far deeper than mere formal oversight of order and doctrine. All the Epistles are shot through with a profound sense of mutual love and compassion between Apostle and his people. To his brothers and sisters in Christ in Philippi Paul writes:

> "It is right for me to feel this way about all of you, since I have you in my heart and, whether in chains or defending and confirming the gospel, all of you share in God's grace with me. God can testify how I long for all of you with the affection of Christ."[85]

I thought long and hard about whether my attachment to the Romanies had become more about having my own needs met than about the call to an apostolic ministry. It is clear, from Paul's letters, that his affection for those he had led to faith is inseparably woven into his devotion to Christ. His loving relationships with his people derived from their shared vocation to be co-workers in God's vineyard. They were a missionary people serving a missionary God. Jesus was the vine and they the branches; his lifeblood was transmitted through the whole vine. Keeping in step with the Holy Spirit meant keeping Jesus central.

---

[84] Acts 20:13-38

[85] Philippians 1:7-8
NB. "I have you in my heart" [TNIV] can equally well be translated "you hold me in your heart" [NRSV]. Thus the subject and object of the love are interchangeable in the Greek suggesting full reciprocity in the relationship between Paul and the Philippian believers. The Amplified Bible captures this well:
"It is right and appropriate for me to have this confidence and feel this way about you all, because you have me in your heart and I hold you in my heart as partakers and sharers, one and all with me."

Only in this way could the bonds of love between missional leader and his missional people remain wholesome and fruitful. This was no ordinary human attachment. This was something beyond what the Greeks called *phileo* love. This was *agape* love, a Christ-like love, a love that was willing to sacrifice all for the sake of the mission. In that spirit, I began to explore, whether there might be any way in which some kind of ongoing contact with the Romanies might be possible... or even permissible.

Chapter twenty-nine

Exiles

"They are kept in the world as in a prison-house, and yet they are the ones who hold the world together."[86]

Moses – Martin - Roy

As this narrative begins to draw to an end and I prepare to move on to new pastures, I continue to reflect on these common bonds of love and affection of which I have written and which are always at the heart of any missionary movement of the Spirit. Missionary and new believer naturally draw close to one another because of their shared life in Christ. But, within each story, it may be possible to identify areas of common ground that have given rise to the deep feelings of empathy which have proved so important in the journey of spiritual renewal.

---

[86] David Bosch, *Transforming Mission* 1991 p.48

At the surface level, I have almost nothing in common with my Romany friends other than our shared faith. Our cultural background and education are utterly different. And yet, at a deeper level, I have come to understand that there is something significant that we do have in common. It is the experience of being *exiles*.

In my own life, I have, for some years, felt a kind of double exile. I feel exiled both from the prevailing culture of secular humanism, *and* from the culture of the institutional church. In 2007 this crystallized in a picture I received when praying one day.

> I saw in my mind's eye two huge wheels. They were linked by cogs and were only managing to turn very laboriously because they had rusted up. I saw myself labouring to keep the wheels turning and calling on colleagues to oil the machinery. But this oil brought only a temporary ease in the system. Meanwhile, down at ground level, a spinning top was turning fast and effortlessly in its gyroscopic three-dimensional orbit. Every now and then it would run up against the huge rusting cogs and its life would be endangered for a few seconds before it recovered its own internal movement again.

Reflecting on this image, I came to understand the two huge wheels as MODERNITY and CHRISTENDOM. These two movements had held sway for centuries but now, as we were turning our way into the third Millennium, they were both beginning to run out of steam and grind to a halt. Because of the huge momentum generated by the scale of these projects, the machinery still had life in it, but that life was becoming ever harder to sustain.

Enlightenment rationalism had arisen in Europe in the eighteenth century as a radical new way of thought that promised to explain everything in existence by the application of pure logic. Huge advances were made in science and technology of which we are the heirs. However, it took two world wars to finally convince our race that pure reason, unchecked by love, had the capacity to turn in on itself and destroy the very things we secretly valued the most. People began to search for something beyond Modernity.

Meanwhile, the institutional churches of the developed world had arisen out of an alliance between state and church. Emperor Constantine had incorporated the Christian faith into the Roman Empire in the fourth century in the hope that the church would be the leaven in society. However, all too often, the church was compromised by the prevailing values of the secular world and the New Testament vision of church was lost within an increasingly hierarchical and bureaucratic machine.

It came as a kind of confirmation of my picture when, one day, I spotted the latest slogan for the Alpha course. This bore an astonishing likeness to the two huge wheels turning. The Alpha slogan suggested powerfully, that you cannot engineer authentic love in a factory. There is always more to life than what science and reason can deliver up.

At a deep level, I came to believe that the institutional church had increasingly bought into the ideals of secular democracy and was running the risk of selling its birthright to modernity. The work of the Holy Spirit was so collapsed into the bureaucratic machine as to forfeit any sense of sovereignty or spontaneous freedom. The church's centre of gravity had become the agenda-and-minutes-driven work of a council of people chosen, not because they were filled with the Spirit and passionate about the Kingdom of God and mission, but because they liked meetings. Looking back to his American homeland from the African plains, Vincent Donovan saw clearly what had gone wrong:

> "There are many idols, but two which, I believe, particularly mesmerize the Western church, are individualism on the one hand, and love of organization on the other".[87]

The first thing that he felt had got lost along the way was the authentic experience of Christian community. The second consequence was that the church was turning in on itself and losing it vocation to be a blessing to the world. Donovan's indictment is absolute:

> "An inward turned Christianity is a dangerous counterfeit,
> an alluring masquerade.
> It is no Christianity at all". [88]

---

[87] Vincent J. Donovan – *Christianity Rediscovered – An Epistle from the Masai 1978, 1982* page 89
[88] Page 104

The effect of all of this on the centrifugal apostolic ministry of the church is catastrophic. The church simply begins to turn in on itself. Donovan captures perfectly the net in which the parish priest finds himself caught:

> "We have become in truth a temple people once again, with our whole Christian life, such as it is, revolving around a parish church building. Much more than we care to admit, our vitality is measured and judged by just how well we keep up and maintain that temple and its surrounding grounds and institutions. Our very notion of priest or pastor is built up from his connection with that building. Many years of his life are devoted to its upkeep, and our judgment on his value is based largely on the manner in which he carries out sacred actions, sacerdotal actions, sacrificial actions in that sacred building."[89]

And so, I found myself to be in a double exile, estranged from the prevailing culture of the world and estranged from the bureaucratic, building-and-meeting-based institution that I felt the church had become. Although Donovan's context as a missionary to the Masai tribes of Tanzania was quite different to mine as parish priest in rural Kent, his experience of isolation rang loud bells for me:

> "... a missionary is essentially a *social martyr,* cut off from his roots, his stock, his blood, his land, his background, his culture. He is destined to walk forever a stranger in a strange land. He must be stripped as naked as a human being can be, down to the very texture of his being. Paul said Christ did not think being God was something to be clung to, but emptied himself, taking the form of a slave. He was stripped to the fibre of his being, to the innermost part of his spirit. This is the truest meaning of poverty of spirit. This poverty of spirit is what is called for in a missionary, demanding that he divest himself of his very culture, so that he can be a naked instrument of the gospel to the cultures of the world."[90]

---

[89] Page 140
[90] Page 194

Donovan makes clear that there is a very real - and indeed necessary - price that those engaged in apostolic ministry have to pay. The experience of exile is a necessary consequence of missional work.

But what about the Romanies? Were they not also resident aliens in contemporary Britain, living out a pattern of life that sat very uncomfortably alongside the both the dominant secular culture *and* the culture of the church? Their experience of exile has strong resonances with that community of Jews that King Nebuchadnezzar had placed in ghettoes in Babylon in the sixth century BC. For it was precisely there, in exile, that the Jews had been forced to ask deep, searching question regarding their own identity; it was there that they had rediscovered their own heritage; and it was there that God had breathed His Spirit into their dry bones and reformed them into a people after His heart. I was witnessing a similar process of spiritual renewal taking place within the exiled Romany community of Cranbrook.

Over recent years, I had been greatly encouraged to reflect on my own sense of isolation and exile through the writings of a variety of commentators, and notably the American Old Testament scholar, Walter Brueggemann. He likens the condition of the disciple, trying to live out the faith in the context of the contemporary American church, to that of the Jewish exiles of old. Interestingly, Luther had described the Roman Catholic Church of his day as in a state of "Babylonian Exile"! My reading around this theme helped me to make sense of my own experience and to begin to understand it in a creative way. Private study was helpful, but the real turning point came when I found in the Romanies, kindred spirits, folk who shared the same longing for purpose and meaning in their lives as I did, and who shared the same struggle to find their place in the context in which they were living out their lives.

There were two things, however, that the Romanies embodied that I had never experienced before. Firstly, their way of living out the Gospel with each other seemed entirely authentic to their own Romany culture. Secondly, their culture reflected, in remarkable ways, the pattern of community that Jesus formed around himself when on earth. A community that is at once intimate and open is hugely attractive and compelling to anyone who has lost faith in the atomized and individualistic life of contemporary Britain. The Romanies and I shared the same profound experience of exile; but their culture had succeeded in protecting them from the very forces that had robbed me of an authentic experience of the kind of community Jesus had come to earth to create. It was all this that had drawn me so irresistibly to share my own life with them.

This brings me to a further remarkable twist in the story that we shared. During the early summer of 2008 another small group of exiles started coming to St Dunstan's. These were three Afghan boys who were seeking asylum in Britain on account of the religious persecution they had experienced in their home country. These young lads quickly made a home with us and began to learn English. They shared the same deep longing for baptism as the Romanies and, like them, were keen for it to be by full immersion. I am convinced that one of the reasons they bonded so delightfully with the Romanies was their common experience of cultural isolation. Although for quite different reasons, the Romanies, the Afghans and I were all exiles, all seeking truth and meaning in a strange and often hostile world.

After a few months the boys were moved on to Canterbury where they were given accommodation and could receive an education. There they met up with others sharing the same plight, who we quickly became friendly with. They travelled over to Cranbrook, week by week, to share in the Friday Romany Cluster and, over the months, deep friendships were formed between the two groups. One young lad has been welcomed into one of the Romany families as though he were one of their own.

Moses & Sohrab

154

A climax for all of us, was the evening when twelve were confirmed by Bishop Stephen in Canterbury Cathedral. At the time of writing, the Afghan boys are being nurtured by St Mary Bredin, the church in Canterbury where I had served as a curate before moving to Cranbrook. As asylum seekers, they are facing long interviews at the Home Office where they have to attempt to prove that they are practicing Christians and that any decision to send them back to their home country would be to send them back to their deaths. And yet, life for them in Britain is tough. Two of them were the victims of a violent attack by masked thugs in their home in Canterbury. This was almost certainly an act of religious hatred, as the boys' bible was torn up in front of their eyes as they lay on the floor.

As well as bonding with the Afghan boys, the Romanies bonded in a remarkable way with another group who came to Cranbrook. These were the teenaged children from Uganda who sang in the marvellous *Hope Africa* choir. On their second visit to St Dunstan's three of the Romany families each hosted two or three Ugandan children in their homes and instantly found themselves on the same kind of common ground that they had discovered with the Afghans. Months later some of them are still emailing each other.

All this reminded me of that marvellous description of the early Christians written by a contemporary historian living a century after Jesus had been on earth. There is a timeless feel to these words. They capture perfectly the paradoxical experience of the disciple who, like Jesus, lives in this world but is aware they are not of it. This is the experience of the exile, of the resident alien…

> "For the Christians are distinguished from other men neither by country, nor language, nor the customs which they observe. For they neither inhabit cities of their own, nor employ a peculiar form of speech, nor lead a life which is marked out by any singularity. The course of conduct, which they follow has not been devised by any speculation or deliberation of inquisitive men; nor do they, like some, proclaim themselves the advocates of any merely human doctrines. But, inhabiting Greek as well as barbarian cities, according as the lot of each of them has

determined and following the customs of the natives in respect to clothing, food, and the rest of their ordinary conduct, they display to us their wonderful and confessedly striking method of life.

They dwell in their own countries, but simply as sojourners. As citizens, they share in all things with others and yet suffer all things as if foreigners. Every foreign land is to them as their native country, and every land of their birth as a land of strangers. They marry, as do all others; they beget children; but they do not destroy their babies. They share their table with all, but not their bed with all. They are in the flesh, but they do not live after the flesh. They pass their days on earth, but they are citizens of heaven. They obey the prescribed laws, and at the same time surpass the laws by their exemplary lives. They love all men and yet are persecuted by all. They are unknown and condemned; they are put to death and restored to life. They are poor yet make many rich; they are in lack of all things and yet abound in all; they are dishonoured and yet in their very dishonour are glorified. They are evil spoken of and yet are justified; they are reviled and bless; they are insulted and repay the insult with honour; they do good yet are punished as evildoers. When punished, they rejoice as if quickened into life; they are assailed by the Jews as foreigners and are persecuted by the Greeks; yet those who hate them are unable to assign any reason for their hatred. To sum it all up in one word—what the soul is to the body, that are Christians in the world." [91]

---

[91] The Epistle to Diognetus c. AD 130

Chapter Thirty

A Second Naivety[92]

"Truly I tell you,
unless you change and become like little children,
you will never enter the kingdom of heaven."[93]

"Like newborn babies, crave pure spiritual milk,
so that you may grow up in your salvation
now that you have tasted that the Lord is good."[94]

The call of the Gospel to every disciple is a call to grow into the full stature of Christ. It is a most lovely paradox of the message of Jesus, that in order to grow up, we have to become like little children. Peter, who walked for three years alongside his master, went a step further when he wrote in his epistle that, in order to grow up, we had to become like newborn babies. Sharing my life with the Romanies brought me face to face with this truth. Whilst I have more religious information in my head than they will probably ever have, I had to recognize that, in all their simplicity of faith, they were often much closer to the kingdom of heaven than I. Whilst my faith had become ever more complex and nuanced, theirs is uncluttered and child-like. With some measure of sorrow I could remember the early days following my conversion when I was twenty-five. Back then I was in the full flush of what I would now call a *first naivety*, a kind of sustained honeymoon period when a whole new world of faith was opening out before my eyes. As the years rolled on, something of that first naivety began to fall away and I entered a protracted period characterized by uncertainty, confusion and perplexity. I had lost something of my first joy. I had forfeit my *first naivety*. The experience of cancer in 2000 turned everything upside down. As I emerged from eighteen months of treatment my centre of gravity had shifted from my head to my heart and I found myself in

---

[92] The French post-modern philosopher, Paul Riceour, wrote of a second naivety.
[93] Matthew 18:3
[94] 2 Peter 2:2

search of a *second naivety.* I knew it was impossible to go back and pretend the simplicity of faith I had once known; I had to move on and discover a fresh way forward. I recognized, my faith journey would always be informed, by all I had experienced and learnt thus far. But I had come to see, that experience and learning of themselves, do not necessarily go hand in hand with spiritual progress. Sometimes, too much study can result in scepticism, cynicism, crippling complexity and endless compromise.

An essay by Brueggemann I had read years earlier at theological college promised a pathway through the labyrinth of life. Psalm One, he argued, was faith in all its original innocence, the *first naivety.* As the Psalter unfolds, the reality of life begins to bite and the psalmist has to wrestle to keep his head above water. A turning point comes in Psalm 73 verse 22 when he comes to see that he has been but a "brute beast" all along. There, in the sanctuary of the Lord, the Psalmist begins to glimpse a new way forward. The corner is turned, but it is not until he reaches the final Psalm150, that he re-discovers his original peace and joy and he is able to lift his heart in unadulterated praise. This is the *second naivety.* It possesses all the joy of the *first naivety* but bears the stigmata that life has inflicted.

Sharing my life with the Romanies allows no day to pass where there is a dull moment. As I type these words, Pashey has come on the phone to tell me that she has a new song on her heart that the Lord had given her the previous evening. She sings it to me over the phone. The words are in a very gentle, intimate style, and seem to be speaking directly into my train of reflection. I will allow the song to pick up the narrative…

"See me, how my life it goes,
see me, and how I looked before.
Just believe in Him,
and He will make you see
all the love that your heart wants to know.

Jesus will be calling to you, deep inside your heart.
Let Him be the one to love you more.
He will raise you and keep you for eternity.

Let Him be the one to love you more.
Ho-o-o-o…

Jesus, you are the Prince of Peace
And I want to receive you more.
I want you to live in me, for me to live in you
And I want to love you more.
I sought you and I found you
And I followed you every step of the way
And that's why I am the person I am today.

Jesus will be calling to you…

Believe me, just to hear His voice
and in your heart you will know
Jesus will be calling to you…

He will hold you in His hands
He already has His plans
Let Him be the one to love you more.

He will keep you and raise you for eternity
He's the one to eternal life.
If you will seek Him
Then you shall find Him
And the rest will come.

Jesus will be calling to you…

Jesus I believe in you
And my heart is filled with your love
And now I want to share it to every one
Like the bird of a dove.
Let me be the one to love you more.
I will be waiting for you
Here inside my heart
And let me be the one to love you more.
"See me, how my life it goes, see me, and how I looked before…"

The opening words of Pashey's song pick up on the journey of life, past … present… future… The secret to the search for rest is simply to allow the life of Jesus to emerge from within… *"Let Him be the one to love you more"*. This suggests to me that the way of *naivety*, the way of the child, is about letting go of all struggle for progress, of any desire to have measurable outcomes. It is about receiving life as a gift on a moment-to-moment basis, rather than grasping it and trying to control it.

During these days my Romany friends are receiving songs and revelations of God and feeding them through to me in awe and wonder. Their *naivety* keeps them constantly alert to unexpected, unplanned *kairos* moments of disclosure. Their spirits are attuned to the voice of the Holy Spirit and he comes and goes like the wind, "like the bird of a dove", sovereign and free.

There is something wonderfully childlike about this; but there is also a kind of *spiritual intelligence* here. It is a kind of intelligence quite different to the IQ that is so revered amongst the educated of my culture. We are in awe of the person with high IQ. In recent times, we may have begun to recognize the importance of *emotional intelligence*, but we

Annie & Charlene

have yet to recover an understanding of *spiritual intelligence*. It has been lost from our culture over the centuries and we have become highly educated in one part of our being, but spiritually dumb in another. We cannot go back into the womb again, as Nicodemus pointed out to Jesus[95], but we can be born again of the Spirit. Perhaps, for some of us, this second birth is a birth into a *second naivety*.

I am reminded of the goose in one of Kierkegaard's parables, who flies off one day from the farm where he lives and discovers another world out there of which he had known nothing. He returns to his fellow geese back home and tries to explain to them what he has experienced. In vain he searches for the right words. My discovery of a *second naivety* has been rather like this as I move between two worlds and try to bring something of the wonder of the new place into the familiar of the old. Jesus was aware that his disciples had yet to be born again of the Spirit. You might say, they had yet to fly away from the farm and discover a new world out there. He spoke of a time when this would be fulfilled for them. Then, he promised, "rivers of living water will flow from within them."[96] The Romany Creed that my friends had written began with the words, "We believe Jesus' love is like a running stream..." Faith for them is not something static. It is flowing water, forever on the move. It runs everywhere, even into the desert.

As I began to share ever more deeply in the Romanies' experience of faith, something quite new began to stir within me. Spontaneous emotional engagement is quite natural and every-day for a child. But for an adult, especially a male adult living in Kent, it is seen as a sign of weakness and immaturity. I think the first occasion I became aware that something was shifting within me was at Roy and Pashey's wedding, when I found myself unable to continue reading the vows. I did not decide to weep. I received it as a gift. From then on, when I found myself deeply moved by something, the same thing would happen. It would arise quite gently and spontaneously from somewhere deep within. The Romany girls would say, "Martin's become all emotionable." It was as though they had helped me to find the on/off switch that controlled the release of emotion. My culture had trained me so well to keep the

---

95 John 3:4
96 John 7:38-39

switch off, that I had forgotten where it was located. On one occasion I was showing some of the women photos from my childhood. I came to photos of my brothers Philip and Stephen, who had died all those years ago. For the first time since their deaths, I began grieve freely and openly for them. Rather than a regression into childish ways, it felt like I was becoming more fully human, more mature. I now find myself receiving the gift of tears when on my own, walking, driving, praying. Often one of our songs is there on my heart, if not on my lips. Jesus told the Samaritan woman at the well that something a little like this would happen within the heart of every believer in days to come. He promised a "spring of water" that would "well up to eternal life." [97]

Often, tears now well up from within me simply as a response of awe and wonder at what God is doing and a sense of privilege of being caught up in a fresh move of the Spirit. As Jesus had said, "Blessed are the eyes that see what you see. For I tell you, many prophets and kings wanted to see what you see but did not see it, and to hear what you hear and did not hear it."[98] Tears also arise as a response to a wave of compassion. Part of the gift is simply the ability to begin to let go of my own myriad agendas and to enter the life-stream of the other.

A wonderful description of this can be found in Sebastian Faulkes's book, *Human Traces.* He unfolds the story of a young French man who is about to graduate from years of medical training and begin his work as a doctor. He is travelling along in a coach when, out of the blue, he finds himself caught up in an unexpected wave of compassion for a peasant woman travelling with him…

> "He looked back to the woman in her dark corner of the coach and felt a profound and disabling emotion pour through him. He had lost his sense of her as a second person, a source of minor irritation, and experienced a sudden and irresistible feeling of identity with her. It was more than sympathy, something far less polite; it seemed as though his blood was in her veins and that her despair was the charge that animated his perception of the world. Her position was hopeless; he was obliged to bear

[97] John 4:14
[98] Luke 10:23-34

her pain; both of them were connected in some universal, though unseen, pattern of humanity. His obligation was not to diagnose her but to love her; while his greater duty was to the larger reality, that place outside time where their connection had been made, the common ground of existence into which he had been granted a privileged glimpse." [99]

His experience is at once profoundly simple and utterly transformative. For, by the time the young man steps out of the coach, he has determined to sell his medical instruments and begin training to be a priest. This piece of literature helped me enormously both to make sense of what I was experiencing with the Romanies, and of my own ordination. Rabbi Abraham Heschel captures something very similar:

> "There is a loneliness in us that hears. When the soul parts from the company of the ego and its retinue of petty conceits; when we cease to exploit all things but instead pray the world's cry the world's sigh, our loneliness may hear the living grace beyond all power." [100]

As the experience of tears began to become a normal pattern for me, I started to wonder if this was a kind of window into the heart of God. If this is how I was feeling for a certain person, or group of people, then this must surely be how God is feeling at all times, for everyone. The feelings of compassion I was experiencing were a mere drop in the ocean of compassion within the heart of God. The love I feel for this person, is the same love that Jesus feels for the whole world. And here came the crunch. For I became only too aware that my love was not like Jesus' love in an important way. I had yet to learn to love my enemies. And this I recognized was a key test of the authenticity of my discipleship. Fortunately, God is still working on my case.

We tend to understand the gift of tears as a pastoral gift. To get alongside someone at a deep level, compassion is, of course, an essential. I came to recognize, however, that there has to be more to it than this. Key questions began to formulate as I examined my inner motives. To what

---

[99] Sebastian Faulkes *Human Traces* 2006 p.15
[100] Rabbi Abraham Heschel *God in search of Man* 1955

extent was this ministry to the Romanies more about having my own needs met than those of the other? And, more importantly still, what was the ultimate goal of this ministry? For, all too easily, the whole force of this love could become inward looking, self-serving, and yes, ultimately, tribal. When the life of a community becomes *centripetal* it rotates increasingly around its own in-house agendas. Gradually, without noticing what is happening, this kind of communal life can so turn in on itself that, ultimately, it destroys itself.

As I searched my way through these fears, I felt it important to have a fresh look at those occasions when Jesus wept. It was immediately clear to me that there was far more going on here than what we call "pastoral sensitivity". Right at the centre of Jesus' experience was a clear missional impulse. Through events on the ground, especially tragic events, the glory of God would be revealed, the Kingdom would advance, and the mission would move on to its next stage. The tears that Jesus shed at the grave of Lazarus, his friend, were - in the first instance - a spontaneous response to the tragedy of the moment. Jesus shared deeply the oceans of grief that were sweeping through the little village of Bethany. But those tears were also directed towards the horizon of God's future. He wept to see the dawning of the Kingdom of God. And so those tears became the source of power. They were the seedbed of both compassion and dynamic action. Moments after Jesus calls Lazarus from his tomb, a series of events unfold which lead, ultimately, to the cross and the resurrection, to the salvation of the world. Jesus' tears of compassion were thus *centrifugal* in their force, outward looking, missional in their intent.

These reflections began to inform my work with the Romanies. It was as though Jesus was passing to me a pair of bi-focal spectacles. One moment I was to focus fully on what was happening before my eyes. The next moment I was to shift my focus to the horizon of God's future, to the mission that he was calling all of us to join in. Here, the triangle I had shared at our weekend away was a useful tool. We were learning how to achieve the right balance between devotion to God [UP], care within the community of faith [IN], and mission to the world [OUT]. At best, we experience these three dimensions as one single, sovereign move of the Holy Spirit. This is the pattern we find in the life of the early church as it unfolds from Pentecost. Paul often writes of his "many tears".[101] He weeps as he longs for Christ to be more fully formed within the churches he has planted. He weeps for the saving grace of Jesus to be made known to those who do not yet belong. He weeps also for those who oppose his work. But Paul's tears are not self-indulgent. They are a response to his sorrow for those who remain blind to what God is doing.

Tears are, of course, of their very nature, spontaneous. When Jesus invites us to become like little children, his invitation is to recover that childlike spontaneity that we have forfeit over the years. In our *first naivety* we weep, laugh, dance and play as the Spirit stirs up the waters within us. When we forfeit our first joy, we become like those Pharisees and Scribes of Jesus' day, who would not mourn when a dirge was played and would not dance when the pipe was played.[102] Neither the austere ministry of John the Baptist nor the exuberant style of Jesus was acceptable to them. And so they remained, for Jesus, "whitewashed tombs", [103] unable to move on, unable to rediscover their long-lost *first naivety*. However, those who did receive Jesus, grew up into a maturity in him which was remarkably child-like and free. These disciples were granted the right to become "children of God".[104] This is the kind of life that we read about in the New Testament, where growth comes quite spontaneously and flows on inexorably, like a river. As the church of Jesus Christ sprang into life, pharisaical Judaism turned in on itself and remained an inward-looking sect with no future.

Life amongst the Romanies is characterized above all else by spontaneity. One Friday as about thirty of us we were singing and dancing together, we felt - quite suddenly - that we did not need to remain cooped up in the small room at Church House. Instead of continuing to dance in a circle we moved on out of the building and right down onto the High Street, singing and dancing all the way with Margareta, my wife, keeping us more or less together with her accordion. Any attempt to

---

[101] 2 Corinthians 2:4; Philippians 3:18;
cf. Acts 20:19; 2 Tim 1:4; Psalm 19:136; Psalm 126:5;
[102] Matthew 11:17
[103] Matthew 23:27
[104] John 1:12-13

have planned this into an "order of service," would probably have killed it dead. The time had to be right, and the right time would not be a matter of planning, but of discerning when the *kairos* moment had arrived and then, like little children, quite literally going with the flow. This spontaneous happening was an outward expression of an inner joy which had arisen within each of us and which we all shared in. It was something sacramental, pointing beyond itself to the unseen reality of God, to the eternal dance of the Trinity. For the Romanies it was an entirely natural manifestation of community life. But, in truth, it probably needed a dancing vicar around the place to bestow upon it an official blessing. Moses commented afterwards that it had been the best bit of the evening for him.

Rolland Allen writes about this kind of thing in a remarkable chapter entitled *"The Nature and Character of Spontaneous Expression."*[105] He comments that "…this unexhorted, unorganized, spontaneous expansion has a charm far beyond that of our modern highly organized missions." His thesis is that the reason the Early Church enjoyed such success was precisely because of the child-like spontaneity of the first believers. Children have an inherent gift to enthuse others and draw them into play. But, as we grow up, the need to control and organize begins to rob us of our first joy. As our godly play begins to fall away, we forfeit the very thing we valued most. Allen identifies fear as the culprit:

> "Whether we consider our doctrine, or our civilization, or our morals, or our organization, in relation to a spontaneous expansion of the Church, we are seized with terror, lest spontaneous expansion should lead to disorder." [106]

Like Allen, not a few of us have come to despair of the iron yoke of institutionalism that has been placed on our shoulders. Although writing nearly a century earlier, Allen captures both my exasperation and my hope:

---

[105] Rolland Allen *The Spontaneous Expansion of the Church and the causes which hinder it.* 1927   Chapter 2 *The Nature and Character of Spontaneous Expression*
[106] P. 13

"I must acknowledge that to sigh after an inefficient simplicity is vain, and worse than vain. But if we, toiling under the burden of our organizations, sigh for that spontaneous freedom of expanding life, it is because we see in it something divine, something in its very nature profoundly efficient, something which we would gladly recover, something which the elaboration of our modern machinery obscures and deadens and kills." [107]

Allen identifies here the principle reason for our loss of the divine spark. It is our craving to have order. But the wonderful paradox is that, when spontaneity flows unfettered and God-breathed, the result is not chaos but glorious new life! Should we be surprised? After all, it was out of chaos that the *ruach* Spirit of the Lord breathed creation into existence at the beginning of time. And it is a creation shot through with endless surprises; a creation that continues to unfold as we allow God to be God and to continue to amaze us. This is not something I would ever attempt to teach to a Romany any more than I would attempt to teach a child to play. Play for them is in the blood. They are our teachers. And that is why this book is "an Epistle *from* the Romanies."

Pashey

<hr>

[107] P. 7

Chapter Thirty-One

The Pure in Heart

"Blessed are the pure in heart, for they shall see God!" [108]

Cranbrook – Spring 2009

As this Epistle from the Romanies now draws to a close and I prepare to move on to Luton, it is abundantly clear that God has far from finished in his dealings with them. As part of my sabbatical, Margareta and I spent ten days on pilgrimage in the Holy Land in early February 2009. For some weeks prior to our departure, I had been priming Pashey and Moses to take on the leading of the Friday evening Cluster during my absence. We all knew that the future of this work was largely dependant on their ability and willingness to take the baton that I was passing to them and run with it. I had no doubt about their ability; in fact I told them that I, as a *gorgia,* would never be able to lead the Romanies forward in faith as well as one of their own could. My fears centered around whether they would have the self-discipline to actually make it happen week by week. The shadow side of their spontaneous culture – when things happen only if "God is willing" – was that they would sometimes decide God wasn't willing simply because it wasn't convenient for them! The ability to organize, I told them, was the one thing I, as a *gorgia,* had to offer them. I knew how to make things happen. Would they be able to keep the show on the road without me?

Almost as soon as I had set foot on firm ground at Heathrow following our arrival home from Israel, my mobile rang and there was Annie telling me, how her family had been struck by a horrible virus, with little Moses being taken to hospital. I thought that would have been enough to stop the Friday meetings. But then Charlotte came on the phone, bursting with excitement, telling me how her dad, Moses, had led the first Friday meeting and had, according to all reports, done it brilliantly, even finding a singing voice he never knew he had. On the

---

[108] Matthew 5:8

following Friday Moses and Pashey had led the evening together, having chased up their people so effectively that over thirty came along. Hallelujah! My soul sang. I had done myself out of a job. The birth of indigenous Romany leadership at this critical point was just as significant as all the signs and wonders and all the baptisms that we had seen since summer 2008.

There were further lovely developments. Lottie's partner, Mark, had decided to be baptised. Mark had been rather on the fringe of all that had been happening. But he had been moved by all the prayer, that had gone up for his son and by the compassion and love within the Romany community. As fourteen-year-old Charlene had put it to me, "the music went through him." As a non-Romany, his coming on board was especially significant. The blessing was now passing from the Romanies on to others in the most natural way. To crown it all, Mark and Lottie decided the time had come to get married and so we all look forward to a great celebration in a few months time.

Meanwhile, the three sisters, Lottie, Rachel and Naomi, were rejoicing that their brother, Levi, had just been released from prison. The last time I had seen Levi was as part of the crew of Romanies who had cleared the oak in the vicarage garden. At that time, Levi had been addicted to heroin and was about to enter a long prison term. Now, here he was standing before me as though born again. In prison he had been through to hell and back as he came off heroin cold turkey. Guided by the prison chaplain he had then re-discovered his faith, which had begun in his youth when Pastor Lywood had baptised him in Goudhurst. At the time of his entry to prison there was no Romany community of faith in place to hold him. But how wonderful now, a year and half later, that his close relations had formed a strong Christian web of love within which he could continue to grow. That same web was there to receive Reuben when, a few weeks later, he also came out of prison having discovered faith in Jesus there. His sister, Pashey had not seen him for over two years. I think all this played a part in stirring the heart of Pashey's father, Reuben. It had meant everything to see God at work in the life of his son Reuben, now on the straight and narrow. Big Reuben had been led to faith, thirty-five years earlier by Pastor Lywood. It was my privilege now to baptise him just days before moving on to Luton. There was great joy in the Romany community as we saw God begin to pour out his blessings on the older generation.

Martin, Reuben & his son, Reuben

All the signs are that a number of other deeply needy people who are linked into the life of this tribe will also come to find rest for their souls in times to come. For many months we had been praying fervently for young Kelly Skilton who had been undergoing a radical treatment plan for her leukaemia. She braved the side effects of the chemotherapy and her friends seemed to be always at her side. From time to time her mother, Jane, had been coming along to the Friday meetings. I think the "music went through" Jane too, for as it was going on, she turned to me and said that she wanted to be baptised too! A few moments later I shared it with all the others and a terrific wave of delight washed over us all.

As we had turned the corner into the New Year it seemed that there was a second wave of revelations beginning to unfold. The first wave had begun with Moses' seeing the light from the church tower, Charlotte's experience of the burning bush outside her home, and Pashey's vision of the words "three men swimming" which had come to fulfilment in the baptisms of the Afghan boys who were now very much on our hearts as they continued to seek asylum and build a new life in Canterbury. But there was now a second wave underway, and the fresh revelations were intensifying a question that had been on my heart throughout these days.

Jesus had said, "blessed are the pure in heart, for they shall see God".

These had been the words Pastor Lywood had received from Jesus on the day of his conversion and they had been the source of inspiration that had led to his decades of work with the Romanies. I felt that these words were to be the title of this book. In my reflections, I have tried to explore something of what Jesus meant by "the pure in heart". We have looked at the lovely qualities of simplicity, humility, spiritual openness, compassion, child-like naivety, playfulness and spontaneity that make the Romanies so attractive as a people. We have also explored the possibility that the blessings that have been poured on them have something to do with the special place that vilified, marginalized exiles have within the heart of God. But all this draws us on to look more closely at the second half of Jesus' beatitude:

What does it mean to "see God"?

When the Lord appeared to Moses at the burning bush "Moses hid his face, because he was afraid to look at God." [109] The writer seems to be saying that to look at the fire in the bush is to look at God. In the book of Deuteronomy we read, "God is a consuming fire".[110] For these ancient Hebrews, the closest they came to understanding the nature of the God who was revealing himself to them, was to gaze at the miracle of a bush which was burning but not being consumed by the fire. Yet other passages of scripture seem to challenge this outlook and serve as warnings.

The assembly of Israelites had cried out "let us not hear the voice of the Lord our God nor see this great fire anymore, or we will die." [111]And in the book of Judges when Manoah and his wife experience the sight of a flame blazing up from the altar towards heaven, Manoah cries out to his wife "we are doomed to die! We have seen God!"[112]

---

[109] Exodus 3:6
[110] Deuteronomy 4:24
[111] Deuteronomy 18:16
[112] Judges 13:22

When we move into the New Testament, we find John stating, in both Gospel and Epistle, that "no one has ever seen God"[113] *and yet*, when the Apostle Thomas sees the risen Jesus he declares, "my Lord and my God."[114]

Scripture seems to leave the question of "seeing God" hanging in the air and shrouded in mystery. Perhaps that is just where it should be. For Jesus, only the genuinely "pure in heart" will be open to experiencing God's awesome presence and elusive nature. In my search for understanding, one thing has become increasingly clear. It is only those who are humble and lowly of heart, only those who cry out to God in the midst of their distress for more of him, who come close to glimpsing him. And so I turn to the most recent wave of revelations.

Roy was at first quite reluctant to speak of his recent experience of the risen Jesus. I learnt of it first through his wife, Pashey, who wanted to shout it from the rooftops. Such is the need of those born to perform! However, for some weeks, Roy, pondered these things quietly in his heart, rather like Mary had done during Jesus' childhood. Some weeks later, they sat me down to give me a full account of what had happened one morning in January 2009.

Roy had come back from taking the three older boys to school and told Pashey he was going to go upstairs to lie down and have a rest. He wasn't to reappear downstairs until two hours later, though he had no idea that such a period of time had elapsed. Roy sat down on his bed and began to plead with God that he would be able to "see the Holy Spirit". He had been crying out in this way to God for some months. If the Holy Spirit had appeared in the form of a dove at Jesus' baptism, then it should be possible for this to happen again. After some time praying with his eyes shut, Roy felt the very real presence of a warm hand on his head. Although his eyes were shut, he was aware that Jesus was standing right next to the bed, dressed in white, with long hair. As Roy had been praying to Jesus, so now Jesus was praying for Roy, with his hand on his head. This continued for some time. Then Roy felt the whole bed begin to shake violently. Afraid, he opened his eyes

[113] John 1:18; 1 John 4:12
[114] John 20:28

to see that there was now a very large white bird lying right across the bed, trying to fly off but unable to do so because Roy was leaning over it, almost embracing it. When Roy sat up, the bird rose up, the bed stopped shaking, and the bird disappeared from the room.

I have to say that when I first heard this account, I found myself seeking a psychological explanation for what was clearly a quite profound experience. But Pashey then went on to tell me of something else that had had happened that same morning after Roy had gone upstairs to rest. Their little son, Reuben, just four, had come up to Pashey and said: "Daddy's praying to Jesus and Jesus is praying for daddy. And there is a big mother duck upstairs." Pashey had never heard little Reuben say anything quite like this before and quickly dismissed it as baby talk. It wasn't until Roy came downstairs some two hours later and told her what had happened to him that she realized the significance of her little boy's words. Reuben's "big mother duck" was his way of describing the huge white bird that he had seen in his mind's eye. Both Roy's and his son's experience were real. The one was confirmation of the other. Whatever one might make of this, something quite uncanny was going on. I believe that the huge bird that Roy saw that morning was an answer to his prayer to be granted sight of the Holy Spirit and that the hand on his head was the hand of the risen Jesus. I am not sure that one can come any closer to "seeing God" than this.

Roy's plea to experience the Holy Spirit went hand in hand, for him, with another prayer: to be healed of his chronic insomnia. His brother, Moses, had been healed of his insomnia from the moment the light had shone into his living room that Christmas Eve of 1998 and we are all praying for a similar healing for Roy. So far, that has yet to come. But perhaps the beginning of an answer came that morning when he went upstairs to rest.

Some weeks later, Pashey had a remarkable experience of the Holy Spirit. She awoke at two in the morning with a strong physical sensation of warmth in her heart. Opening her eyes in the darkness of the room she then saw for a few seconds a distinct, small flame hovering over her body. The next morning as she was alone downstairs, getting breakfast ready for the family, she found herself praying quietly in a new language. The Holy Spirit had granted her the gift of tongues.

Once I was back from Israel, Rachel told me of the extraordinary experience she had had while I had been away. Her little Moses had been rushed into hospital with a soaring temperature. Rachel has in recent times experienced extreme anxiety for the wellbeing of her son and, just before leaving to go to Israel I had placed a very light scarf around her neck and we had all prayed for the light yoke of Christ to replace the heavy yoke of terror that was robbing her of peace of mind. When little Moses was rushed into hospital, her anxiety had gone through the roof. She told me how, at one point, she went out to the toilet and there cried out, "Jesus come and help me, I am feeling very weak and vulnerable. Please come and strengthen me!" She then went back to little Moses' bedside feeling just calm enough to pray for him. It was about two hours later when she was still praying, that she saw beautiful, milk-white flakes of snow come very slowly down and pass through her son lying on his bed. It was as though she were seeing the very prayers themselves and the very action of the Holy Spirit, as the flakes of snow were absorbed into his body. Rachel was so astounded by this sight that she prayed to God "Lord, if this is real and not just me imagining it, then please allow the snow to keep on falling like this for two minutes." Her prayer was granted. In the morning the nurse came and took Moses' temperature. It had fallen back to normal. The family went home grateful for the work of the Holy Spirit in their lives. Rachel has since told me that this had been the most powerful experience of God she had ever had in her life. Her family have noticed that Rachel's level of anxiety has fallen significantly and the tablets the doctor had given her have been left on the shelf.

Just a few weeks before this, Charlotte had an experience which, although less sensational than the burning bush she had seen some seven months earlier, was - she felt - more significant. One night, she had been lying, restless, on the sofa downstairs in the living room. Suddenly, she felt a deep sense that she should turn right around so that she would be able to see out of the window at the back of the house. She had the feeling that, if she did so, something important would be revealed to her. Accordingly, Charlotte repositioned herself and began to look out into the dark winter night. A diamond-shaped star appeared. Very gradually, it began to descend in the sky and come to rest. Now, she could see the star through the trees on the far side of the High Street. As with the burning bush, she didn't know why this had happened or what meaning it might have. She simply accepted it as a sign of God's favour, a sign that he was alive and on the move, as he had been when the star from the East had come to rest over Bethlehem at the birth of the saviour.

Finally, I turn to the day in January 2009 on which Marky-boy had had his eye operation in London. This was a day in which all our hearts and minds were focused on what the twelve-year-old lad had to go through. At 7.30 in the morning I walked into the hospital together with Lottie, Mark and their son, Marky-boy. We were later to discover that at the same moment, back in Cranbrook, unbeknown to each other, Pashey and Moses had seen the most extraordinary, vast, glowing golden light emerging from the East as they got up that day. Pashey saw it whilst taking out rubbish to the bins. Moses saw it through his kitchen window. I am still not sure whether this was simply a staggeringly beautiful sunrise, or something beyond that. Those who witnessed it are, however, quite convinced that this was more than a stunning sunrise; it was, they say, far too large for that. It was also a light that was not too bright to look at, and so they felt that it could not be the sun itself. Certainly, of all the revelations the Romanies have spoken to me about, none has filled them with greater awe than this. They were quite ecstatic as they tried to describe it. Pashey even attempted to draw it for me with coloured crayons. In a way, the provenance of the light is of little importance; the question as to whether it was natural or supernatural in its origin was not something they were troubled about. They were happy to leave such academic questions to dualists like me! They were simply bowled over by the sight and spoke of it as though it had been specially arranged for them, as though God were wishing to speak to them through it. There was a clear sense in which it had to be linked with the impending eye operation in London.

During the course of that day, Pashey and Moses felt a new song take shape in their hearts. Moses came up with the words. He shared them with Pashey, who then formed them into a song. That same evening we all gathered together for our Cluster meeting and sang the song for the first time.

"Jesus is a-coming, coming back [3times],
Hallelujah!"

The song has a terrific forward thrust to it, giving birth to a strong sense of anticipation – Jesus is making his way towards us from the future! There are real grounds for hope, whatever our present circumstances might look like. The sense of excitement grew as I explained that the early Christians believed that, when Jesus returns, he will appear like a magnificent sunrise - every eye will turn to the East and behold his glory...

"But for you who revere my name,
the sun of righteousness will rise with healing in its wings.
And you will go out and leap like calves released from the stall".[115]

"He will make your righteousness shine like the dawn,
the justice of your cause like the noonday sun".[116]

Jesus' return would usher in a new age. The old order of sickness and injustice would be swept away and the exiled peoples of God would at last come home. As we celebrated together that Friday evening, suddenly the doors opened and in walked little Marky-boy with bandaged eye, accompanied by mum and dad. How amazing! They had come to celebrate with us all after the ordeal of the day. But there was not a whiff of triumphalism in the room. This was the joy of a people who were discovering that God had come to lift them up, to bless them, and to set them free. This was just a foretaste. The best wine would come at the end. Meanwhile we were learning to live with uncertainty, walking by faith not by sight – would the operation be successful?

Shortly before I moved to begin my new ministry in Luton we took up invitations to take the blessing we had received and share it with other churches. On one Sunday eighteen of us went along to Marden Congregational Church to join with the six or so worshippers there that

---

[115] Malachi 4:2
[116] Psalm 37:6

day. During the service we sang out our blessings, praying that one day that church would be filled again. On the following Sunday fifteen of us headed off to St George's, Deal, one of the large evangelical churches in Canterbury Diocese. Some twenty years earlier they had received a prophecy, that one day the Gospel would impact this country and particularly Kent once again. The prophecy had a particular edge to it:

"The gospel will be brought back to us FROM the outcasts of society".

St George's has experienced wonderful growth in recent times, and now enjoys a most beautifully reordered church building. However, one person commented on the impact the Romanies made on their church that Sunday:

"For all we've got, we haven't got what they've got, and I want it."

Another person went further saying:

"I have the feeling after hearing them, we won't be the same again."

Romany Cluster in Deal

One of their clergy, Shiela Porter, summed up her reflections:

> "As a church we've been asking ourselves over recent weeks why
> we aren't seeing some of the things we read about in the New
> Testament church - why no miracles and manifestations of
> God in the way that those early Christians were blessed. It was
> a like a staleness had set in, in spiritual terms. As the Romanies
> began to share their stories, many of us found ourselves in tears
> as we realized our own poverty. They were such a blessing to
> us in bringing us back to hear from God. For "God chose the
> foolish things of the world to shame the wise; God chose the
> weak things of the world to shame the strong. He chose the
> lowly things of this world and the despised things - and the
> things that are not- to nullify the things that are, so that no
> one may boast before Him. It is because of him that you are
> in Christ Jesus, who has become for us wisdom from God....".
> We heard the challenge to lay down our cleverness and pride
> and come in simplicity as these wonderful people had. On
> Sunday we truly saw the power of God at work and seeing that
> has challenged us to come back to simple faith in Jesus."

Two weeks later we followed up an invitation to take the "sermon slot"
at the church were I had served as a curate, St Mary Bredin, Canterbury.
Twenty-three of us arrived in a convoy of cars and once again there
was great joy all round. It was especially heartening to see all the five
Afghan boys now well established in their new church in Canterbury.
At the service there was one quite remarkable reunion. Ten years earlier
in her pre-Christian days, Pashey had been selling "lucky heather" on
the street in Canterbury. Libby, a member of SMB, got chatting with
Pashey, declined the offer of heather, and then went on to lead Pashey
to faith in Jesus.

*

"Now let thy servant depart in peace.
For mine eyes have seen thy salvation,
A light to the gentiles and glory to Israel".[117]

Like old Simeon in the Temple, I have not seen God. But I have seen his salvation and beheld his glory. And so I am ready to depart. Thank you Romanies! May the Lord keep your hearts pure. You have been greatly blessed. May you continue to be a blessing to others.

*

---

[117] Luke 2:29-32

About the Author

Martin Burrell's first career was as a professional clarinettist. Following studies at Trinity College, Bristol, he was ordained into the Church of England in 1995 and was curate at St Mary Bredin, Canterbury. From 1999 until 2009 Martin was vicar of Cranbrook, Kent. He was then appointed to lead Christchurch, Bushmead, Luton. Both Martin's mother and his wife, Margareta, are from Switzerland. Margareta is a music therapist. They have three children, Rebecca, Naomi and Leo.

Printed in the United Kingdom by
Lightning Source UK Ltd., Milton Keynes
140790UK00002B/12/P